UNTANGLING
THE WEB

St. Martin's Guide

to & LANGUAGE
CULTURE

ON THE INTERNET

UNTANGLING
THE WEB

ST. MARTIN'S GUIDE

TO & LANGUAGE
CULTURE
ON THE INTERNET

Carl S. Blyth
University of Texas at Austin

St. Martin's Press
New York

Sponsoring editor: Robert A. Hemmer
Director of Development: Marian Wassner
Editorial assistant: Simon Glick
Managing editor: Erica T. Appel
Project editor: Deirdre Hare
Art director: Lucy Krikorian
Text design: Dorothy Bungert/EriBen Graphics
Cover design: Evelyn Horovicz

Library of Congress Catalog Card Number: 97-80140

Manufactured in the United States of America.

3   2   1   0   9   8
f   e   d   c   b   a

For information, write:
St. Martin's Press, Inc.
175 Fifth Avenue
New York, NY 10010

ISBN: 0-312-18254-6

Acknowledgments
All screen shots in *Untangling the Web* were located on the Internet, using Netscape. Therefore, the Netscape logo appears throughout. Copyright © 1996 Netscape Communications Corp. Used with permission. All rights reserved. This electronic file or page may not be reprinted or copied without the express written permission of Netscape.

Acknowledgments and copyrights are continued at the back of the book on page 145, which constitutes an extension of the copyright page.

It is a violation of the law to reproduce these selections by any means whatsoever without the written permission of the copyright holder.

To Sarah, Katie, and Claire

Contents

Preface

The Internet is a new and rapidly growing context for cross-cultural communication, and its potential impact on the study and teaching of foreign languages is mind-boggling. For many American students, it is already more common to encounter a foreign language on the Internet than anywhere else. So it makes sense then to study a language in the context in which it is used, including the context of cyberspace. As a general introduction to language and culture on the Internet, *Untangling the Web* can be used profitably with any foreign language textbook, regardless of language or level. *Untangling the Web* was written to provide students with a specialized guide to the Internet as a sophisticated tool to learn a new language and culture.

When we began to explore computer technology as a means to enhance the teaching of foreign languages at the University of Texas at Austin, we quickly discovered that while many students were relatively computer literate and had surfed the Internet before on their own, most of them were unclear about how to use the Internet as a tool to foster their own language learning. *Untangling the Web* was created to bridge this gap. It has three main goals: (1) to introduce students to the incredible foreign language learning resources that are currently available online; (2) to show students ways to use these resources in their own language learning; and (3) to help students learn how to search the Internet for even more foreign language resources.

When integrated into the foreign language curriculum, the Internet can help students grasp the social context of language use. More important, the Internet has the potential to enable my students to communicate in the target language with native speakers in ways unimaginable only a few years ago.

This book was written for everyone who wants to know more about the Internet's applications to foreign language learning. It shows you how to access a plethora of online language learning aids such as bilingual dictionaries, grammars, and test banks. Besides descriptions of pertinent language-oriented material on the Internet, tutorials have been included to give you essential hands-on experience. Chapter 1 includes answers to your most frequently asked questions (FAQs) about the Internet. Chapter 2 explores the hows and whys of surfing the foreign language Web in a step-by-step tutorial. Chapter 3 shows you how to search for and find the riches of the foreign language Internet. In Chapter 4, you will learn about the various online forums for communicating with speakers of other languages. And Chapter 5 gives you an overview of foreign language resources currently available online. Whether you are a foreign language student or teacher, my hope is that this book will help you realize what an amazing tool for language learning the Internet can be in the hands of a savvy user. I look forward to seeing you in cyberspace.

ACKNOWLEDGMENTS

It is fitting that this guide to language and culture on the Internet, the largest communications network in the world, is the product of a network of many friends and colleagues. I would like to thank all my colleagues at the University of Texas at Austin who have encouraged me to explore the potential of emerging technologies for language learning; in particular, my colleagues from the Liberal Arts Media Center and the Department of French and Italian. I am especially indebted to Karen Kelton, Yvonne Munn, and Eric Eubank, whose insights and intuitions about the applications of the Internet to language learning have truly inspired me. I gratefully acknowledge my students, both undergraduate and graduate, who have educated me about which sites are cool and why. I express my deepest gratitude to the wonderful editorial and production staff at St. Martin's Press: to Steve Debow for dreaming up projects while daydreaming of Bali; to Marian Wassner for ferreting out my numerous grammatical infelicities; to Simon Glick for handling a million logistical and editorial details with grace and aplomb; to Dorothy Bungert and Patricia McFadden for their design expertise; to Deirdre Hare for skillfully managing this project under incredible deadlines; and especially to Bob Hemmer for being both an expert reader and an expert friend. And finally, thanks most of all to my good friends Sherry, Keith and Kevin for encouraging me, and to my children—Sarah, Katie, and Claire—for their wonderful, joyful and abundant love. Everyone should have such a support network, online and off.

1 Understanding Internet Basics

Introduction

If you are like most people, you probably find all the hype surrounding the Internet a little bewildering, perhaps even a little intimidating. What's so great about the Internet anyhow? What does the Internet have to offer foreign language learners? And for that matter, what exactly is the Internet?

This book is a friendly guide written for the foreign language learner (and teacher) who wants to know more about the Internet: its concepts, its terminology, its services, and especially its applications to foreign language learning. The main goal of the book is to show you how to exploit the riches of the Internet for your own foreign language learning. Not only will you learn how to access culturally authentic documents in the foreign language that interests you, but you will also discover a plethora of online language learning aids such as bilingual dictionaries, grammars, and test banks. Besides copious explanations and descriptions of pertinent language-oriented material on the Internet, you will also find tutorials that will give you essential hands-on experience.

Beginners are always full of questions but are often afraid to ask them for fear of looking like what they are—beginners! Well, have no fear. In this chapter you will find many of the "frequently asked questions" (FAQs in computer parlance) about the Internet. These questions and answers should help prepare you to start surfing the Internet in no time. Remember though that this chapter covers only the necessary preliminaries, the so-called basics. If you already have some experience with the Internet and feel comfortable striking out on your own, then skip ahead to the other chapters where you can begin surfing!

Can the Internet really help me learn a new language or culture?

Absolutely! Because of its global reach, the Internet is a wonderful tool with which to study modern languages and cultures. Most students who want to improve their knowledge of a language and culture are looking for as much contact with the target language as possible, preferably contact with the native speakers of that language. The Internet allows you to immerse yourself in a language and culture via

1

online authentic, up-to-the-minute documents. It also lets you communicate directly with native speakers of another language. They are usually as interested in learning about your country as you are in learning about theirs. Most foreign language learners and teachers are amazed when they discover the foreign language resources that are currently available online.

What can I do as a foreign language learner with Internet access?

Well, you name it! How you use the Internet to learn more about a foreign language and culture will depend on you—your needs, your interests, and your schedule. You could find a summer job overseas through an international online employment agency, read your favorite foreign fashion, news, or sports magazine, take a virtual tour of a famous art museum such as the Louvre in Paris or the Prado in Madrid. You could read about current events from a foreign news service or peruse the course offerings at a foreign university. Perhaps you would like to talk with native speakers? You could join a foreign language discussion group about something that interests you: World Cup soccer, Tour de France cycling, Italian opera, Japanese stock exchange reports, the German alternative music scene. Whatever it is that interests you, you are likely to find a foreign language discussion group devoted to it. Or, if you would prefer a one-on-one conversation to a group discussion, you could meet a new foreign friend in a cyber café or a chat room, informal places on the Internet where people go to socialize.

If you are more interested in using explicitly pedagogical materials, then the Internet is a good place to go as well. There are many different online language learning resources for you to use: grammar tutorials, fill-in-the-blank vocabulary tests, verb conjugators, pronunciation aids, foreign language dictionaries. You can use these resources in conjunction with a language course you are currently taking or simply on your own to maintain your language skills. In short, as ever more international businesses, universities, and organizations get connected, the Internet affords the foreign language learner many extraordinary opportunities and services.

That sounds great, but what exactly is the Internet?

The Internet is a loosely organized global network of computers that offers many different types of services. If you are on a computer that is connected to the Internet, you can communicate with a staggering number of businesses, organizations, universities, libraries, governmental agencies, and, of course, individuals like yourself. In other words, the Internet allows you to communicate with the world in a way that has never before been possible. And that's not hype, that's fact.

When something is as new as the Internet, it often helps to think about it in terms of something familiar. So try picturing the Internet as a college or university campus, a place where people go to learn about the world. Imagine yourself as a prospective student taking a campus tour. What would you expect the tour guide to say? You would probably anticipate some sort of description of the various buildings according to their general purpose ("This building is used primarily for classrooms and that one for administrative offices") as well as academic disciplines ("On our right is the Department of Spanish and Portuguese and on on our left is Psychology"). In a similar way, the Internet can be characterized in terms of what users can do at various sites and what kind of content or information users will find there. For example, just like students and faculty who go to different places on campus to perform different tasks (relaxing at the student union building, conducting research at the library, listening to a lecture in a classroom), Internet users visit different sites to do different things (send or receive a message, search for information about a topic or person, download software). And similar to the academic departments on campus, Internet sites are often devoted to a specific kind of information, although that information is not always very academic.

While analogies and metaphors are useful in pointing out similarities, they may mask important differences. It is important to remember that the physical spaces of a college campus—the buildings and quadrangles—have no real analog in the world of the Internet. For this reason, the term cyberspace was coined to refer to this brave, new electronic world. While the term Internet refers primarily to the hardware, or the actual infrastructure of networked computers, the term cyberspace is more frequently used to capture the psychological experience of communicating via computer, an experience of being in a curious but exhilarating new social context. With these important differences in mind, it may still be helpful to think of the Internet as a campus with "sites" where you can "go" for different kinds of services and information. In the box below are some of the more important kinds of "places" and services you will find in cyberspace.

Do I need to know a lot about computers to use the Internet?

No, not really. You don't need to be a mechanic to drive a car, do you? Sure, it helps to know some technical details about a car's engine if you plan on owning and using a car. But keep in mind that you will pick up many technical details as you learn to **use** the Internet, and

Important Online Services

World Wide Web: a graphics-based, hypertext linked service that allows you to find information and do research about people, places, events, and topics.
Email (electronic mail): a service that lets you send and receive electronic messages.
Newsgroups: a service that allows you to read and post messages to specific communities of users.
FTP (file transfer protocol): a service that transfers or downloads information from another computer to your own computer or vice versa.
Gopher: a text-only application that guides the user hierarchically to information on the Internet.
Telnet: a service that allows you to log on to another computer from your own computer and to use the other computer as if it were your own.
IRC (internet relay chat): a service that lets people communicate with each other synchronously, or "in real time," often in places called chat rooms.

the goal of this book is to help you do just that. In other words, there's no need to be afraid of the Internet because you don't know much about computers. Once you have a little online experience, you will be surprised how easy the Internet is to use. In fact, the Internet has recently become quite user friendly thanks to the graphic design of the World Wide Web.

What is the World Wide Web (WWW)?

People often use the terms Internet and World Wide Web as if they meant the same thing, but actually they don't. The World Wide Web (also referred to simply as the Web or WWW or W3) is only a part of the Internet, albeit a very important and rapidly growing part. The Web is included in the Internet; it is a smaller network within the much larger Internet network. What makes the Web different from the rest of the Internet is hypertext. Even if you have never heard of hypertext, chances are you've probably already used it. It's nothing more than a text that links to another place in the network, or a text that takes you to another text that takes you to another text. Imagine that you had a stack of numbered notecards. If they were hypertext notecards you wouldn't have to thumb through them in sequential order but could jump to any card at any time—as long as there were links already built in. Card 2 could be linked to card 42, and card 42 to card 15, and so forth. Build enough links and you have yourself a Web.

Unlike other parts of the Internet that are text only, the Web is distinguished by the presence of graphics, photos, sounds, even video—and all are linked! In other words, hypertext links are no longer solely for texts. Today, photos can be linked to other photos, or sounds linked to sounds. In fact, texts, sounds, images, and video can all be linked together in endless multimedia combinations giving rise to what is called "hypermedia." Due largely to its powerful capacity to link various media through hyperlinks, the Web is swiftly replacing other ways of accessing and displaying information on the Internet such as FTP and Gopher. Unlike the static text-only files, WWW documents, commonly called Web pages, are typically highly visual, interactive, and dynamic. Several WWW pages that are all linked together are commonly referred to as a Web site.

While a printed page in a book typically consists of a single block of text that runs from top to bottom, a Web "page" may be divided into several text fields called frames. Frames can contain images or sounds as well as text. Moreover, they usually contain a scroll bar, a device that lets you control which part of the field is displayed on your computer screen. Remember that a Web page—with or without frames—is not really a page at all. This term is just another metaphor used to describe what appears on your screen whenever you are at a specific location or address on the Web. A Web page with frames and scroll bars is shown below.

Figure 1.1

The metaphor of surfing used to describe a television viewer who jumps from channel to channel (channel surfing) is often used to describe the behavior of a Web user who jumps from link to link. Browsing is another metaphor that describes this behavior. The user chooses which link to explore, which text to read, which video to watch. Since there is so much exciting material to explore on the Web, people often surf or browse around until something finally catches their attention. But in order to browse you must first have a Web browser.

A Web browser! What's that?

A browser is the software application that "reads" or displays a Web page. In slightly more technical terms, a browser is software that interprets the computer language that all Web pages or documents are written in. The browser interprets this special Web language, called hypertext markup language (HTML), and then translates it into the display that you see on your computer screen. The two most popular browsers in current use are Netscape Navigator and Microsoft Internet Explorer.

The Web's language, HTML, continues to evolve, just like any language. Web browsers have evolved, too, in order to translate the language as effectively as possible. For example, earlier generations of Web browsers were not "frames capable," that is, they could not display frames. Make sure that your computer has a relatively new version of either Netscape Navigator or Microsoft Explorer. Otherwise, you may not be able to take advantage of all the latest technical developments such as Java script and plug-ins, which will be discussed in full in Chapter 2. The important point to remember about a Web browser is that it is the essential software that allows you to visit or "go to" various sites or addresses on the Web.

How do I go to a site on the Web?

Think of your browser as a taxi driver without the attitude. You "tell" your browser the address of where you want to go by typing it into a small space where your browser says "location" or "address." As long as you know the correct address and you type it in correctly, you can theoretically visit any site on the Web. The technical term for a Web address is uniform resource locator or URL. In essence, a URL indicates the location of a file or document on a certain computer in the network and how to get to it. It is extremely easy to make a mistake when typing URLs because of their length and apparent arbitrariness. Actually, they are not as arbitrary as you may think (you will learn how to decipher the syntax of a URL in Chapter 2). You should be forewarned, however, that while your browser is a very courteous taxi driver, it is very particular about URLs. If you make any mistake whatsoever when typing a URL, the browser will not take you where you want to go. You will most likely get an error message indicating that the file was not found. So pay close attention to a URL's every dot, space, letter, and squiggle.

How do I use a URL that I've only seen or heard about?

You have probably noticed that more and more companies are advertising on the Web. You may have recently seen a television commercial that ended with an appeal to "Visit us on the Web at www-dot-something-dot-com." What does that mean? The commercial is giving you the URL of the company's site on the Web. To find that Web site, just type the URL in your browser's location field. The word "dot" indicates a period ("."). Be sure that your URL starts with "http://" which radio and television ads sometimes leave out. URLs will be discussed in more detail in Chapter 2.

What problems will I encounter?

Well, if you are a beginning language learner and a newbie, that is, new to the Internet, it is probably a good idea to practice in more familiar waters before you start surfing modern language Web sites. Even old pros, however, can run into problems. Many of the difficulties that Internet users encounter are directly related to the massive size of the Internet and its phenomenal growth; it is widely estimated that a million new Internet users are added each month.

At present a common problem with the World Wide Web is wait time, prompting some people to speak of the "World Wide Wait." People tend to forget that the Internet, while very powerful, is still in its infancy. In fact, the Web as we know it today dates back less than a decade. And as with any new technology there are a few bugs to deal with. Don't forget that when you ask your browser to access a file from a server, the computer where that file resides, many other people all over the world may be trying to access the same file. Similar to a telephone switchboard that can only handle a given number of incoming calls at a given moment, a server can only respond to so many hits, or requests for information. When too many people are trying to access the same information, your browser will be unable to connect to the server and will ask you to try again later. So, do what you do when you get a busy signal on the telephone. Wait a while and call back. On occasion, your browser will tell you that the server or computer that you are trying to contact is "down." In this case, you must wait until whatever is wrong with it is fixed. It may be a few minutes or a few hours or a few days. There is often no way of telling.

Will I have to pay long-distance telephone charges to access an international Web site?

No. How you pay for your Internet usage ultimately depends on your Internet service provider (ISP), the entity that controls access to the Internet similar to the way that a phone company controls access to the telephone system. Typically, you will be charged a flat monthly rate for unlimited usage, or you'll be billed by the minute. In either case, the sites you visit in no way affects your fee. Thus, a trip to a Japanese Web site won't cost you any more than a trip across town.

Isn't it true that most Web sites are the electronic equivalent of junk mail?

Well, there is a lot of garbage on the Web. But there is also a lot of terrific material. Unfortunately, the enormity of the Web coupled with its unrestrained growth creates information overload, perhaps the biggest headache of all. Not only is there too much information to be found, but much of it is not accurate, since there currently are no rules or conventions governing what may be published. Because documents published on the Web are not subjected to the normal editorial rigors of the publishing industry, users must carefully evaluate all information accessed on the Internet. When reading a document, the old warning to "Consider the source!" takes on special meaning. To determine whether a document is trustworthy or not, judge first whether its source seems reputable. Where does the document appear? As part of a personal Web site or as part of a large governmental or commercial site? For a complete guide to choosing and evaluating Internet sources, see *Online! A Reference Guide to Using Internet Sources* (St. Martin's Press, 1997) or visit the *Online!* Web site at <http://www.smpcollege.com/online-4style~help>.

And finally, the dynamic nature of the Internet can create problems for users. It is not uncommon for a Web surfer to visit a favorite Web site only to discover that it is no longer there. It has either moved to a new address or disappeared from the Web completely. When a Web site changes address, the new URL may be temporarily posted so that visitors may take note of the change.

How do I get connected? Where do I get equipped?

Getting connected to the Internet is a lot less of a hassle than people think, although some degree of patience is required. There are two kinds of connections to the Internet: direct or indirect (dialup access). On most college campuses nowadays there are computing facilities where one can find computers with direct access to the Internet.

These computers are already configured for Internet access. You will probably need an account in order to log onto these direct access computers. Go to your school's computing center and ask about the procedure for getting Internet access.

If you are connecting from home, things are a little more complicated. You will need four things: a computer, a modem, dialup software, and an Internet service provider. A modem is a device that allows your computer to send and receive information via telephone lines. Just like computers, there are many models of modems to choose from. In general, modems are distinguished by their various speeds, that is, how fast they download information from the Internet onto your computer. If you purchase a modem that is not very fast, you will waste a lot of time waiting for information to load onto your computer. It is recommended that you buy as powerful a modem as you can afford. Note that many newer computers come with built-in modems. You will also need phone dialer software called PPP (point-to-point protocol) or SLIP (serial line Internet protocol) that allows your modem to communicate with other computers.

Next, you must have a Web browser installed on your computer's hard disk. If you use Netscape Navigator or Microsoft Internet Explorer, you should install the more-powerful recent versions. If you are affiliated with an educational institution, you are eligible for free copies of all start-up software (dialup software for your modem and browser software) at your school's computation center.

And finally, you will need a dialup account with your Internet service provider (ISP), the company or educational institution that is responsible for connecting your modem to the Internet. Internet service providers are similar to telephone companies. When you buy a telephone and plug it into a phone jack in the wall, it is not connected. Your phone won't work until you contact the phone company, which then connects your phone to the system (for a fee, of course). Your ISP will connect you, but only if you ask. There are many different ISPs: your school's computer center, a national commercial service, or a nonprofit organization. If you are a college student or faculty member, check with your school's computer center about getting connected. If you are not sure which ISP to use (there are many different providers with various fees and options), consult professional advice at a nearby computer store.

Can my computer get a virus from visiting a Web site?

You should not worry about viruses if you are simply viewing text and images at a Web site. It is possible, however, to pick up a virus by downloading infected software from a Web site. On the other hand, downloading software is usually quite safe as long as the software comes from a respectable source. It is recommended that you install antivirus software on your hard disk to protect yourself against possible viruses whether you use the Web or not. Before downloading any software from a Web site, you should ask yourself whether it is produced by a reputable company.

Can other users find out what sites I visit or what messages I send? How secure is the Internet?

In general, information is not secure on the Internet. There are times when you may be asked to give out confidential information, for example, a credit card number when joining a commercial online service. However, in general, you should think twice before giving out your name, social security number, or credit card number to any individual or company requesting such information via the Web. Can you be sure that the company or individual who is requesting personal information will not sell that information to someone else? Usually the answer is no. You should also be aware that whenever you visit a Web site, you reveal who your Internet service provider is, what site you came from, and what software you are using. The Web site that you visit may also keep track of how long you stay and what parts of the site you explore. Security is also a major issue for email users. It is important to remember that any email message can be copied and rerouted to literally thousands of mailboxes with the touch of a key. In fact, it is possible for a system administrator to read your email messages on your computer. Moreover, while email messages usually arrive at the proper destination most of the time, it is not uncommon for the email to be routed to the wrong mailbox. Therefore, remember that discretion is your best defense against breaches of security. Email will be discussed in greater depth in Chapter 4.

How do I find good foreign language sites?

In order to find something, you need to look. Unfortunately, looking for something on the Internet is like the proverbial search for the needle in the haystack. The trick is to know how to look. In Chapter 3 you will discover how to use two powerful Internet tools—search engines and directories—to locate whatever it is that you are looking for on the Web. Chapter 5 provides a sampler of particularly compelling and innovative foreign language Web sites. The sites described in Chapter 5 are only a fraction of those currently available. They are meant to give you a sense of the incredible diversity and utility of various online foreign language resources.

What if I still have more questions about the Internet?

First of all, you will never use the Internet if you are waiting for the answers to all your questions. In fact, the more you use the Internet, the more questions you will have. Therefore, it is important to learn how to find answers for yourself. Not surprisingly, one of the best places to find information about the Internet is on the Internet. There are several excellent FAQ files, sites organized in a question-and-answer format. One of the best for newbies is Delphi's FAQ file. Visit it at **<http://www.delphi.com/navnet/faq/>**. If you don't find the answer to your question, you can ask them directly via email and they will write you back or post your answer. Another site with general information about using the Internet and World Wide Web can be found at **<http://www.boutell.com/faq/>**. And finally, don't forget that you will find the answers to many of your questions as you work your way through this book's tutorials. For example, in Chapter 2 you will learn how to use your browser's handbook to get online help.

2 Learning to Surf

In Chapter 1 you became acquainted with the Internet—its services and concepts. Now it's time for some hands-on experience. In this chapter, you will learn the basics of operating a Web browser while visiting several language-oriented Web sites. After all, you can't learn how to surf by reading a book. At some point you have to get wet!

This chapter is divided into three parts. The first part is an overview of the popular Web browser Netscape Navigator (version 3.0), including its layout and its major features. While some differences between browsers exist, they all share the same basic functions and layout. As a consequence, what you will learn from using Netscape Navigator will apply to other browsers as well. The second part of this chapter is a tutorial that will teach you most of what you need to know about navigating a Web page. The pages in this tutorial become increasingly sophisticated both in terms of content and technology. And finally, the third part of this chapter is a series of exercises that will allow you to check how well you have digested the major points of the tutorial.

FUNDAMENTALS OF THE WEB BROWSER

This section describes what you see onscreen when using Netscape Navigator, the so-called graphic elements of the browser. When you are using Netscape (or any other browser), your computer screen is divided into two basic parts: the content area and the browser menu and information buttons (see Figure 2.1). The content area is like the screen on a television set. Change the channel and you change the picture. And the browser menu is like the TV's control panel or remote control. The control buttons stay the same regardless of what picture is displayed on the screen. The major components of the Netscape window are:

- title
- menu bar
- toolbar
- location field
- directory buttons

- scroll bars
- status indicator
- progress bar
- mail icon

Title

Every Web page has a title that is displayed just below the menu bar. When you save a Web page on your computer as a file, the file will be identified by the same title.

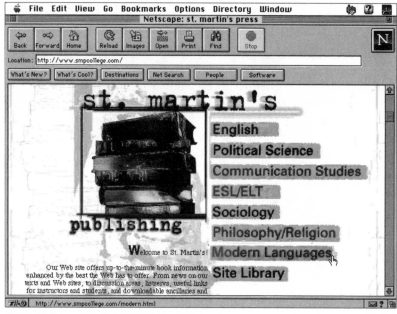

Figure 2.1

Menu Bar

The menu bar appears at the very top of the screen. You access the menu bar by moving the cursor to any word (a menu item) and clicking on it. When you click on a menu item, a pulldown window opens, displaying more choices. These functions listed in the menu bar enable you to perform operations that are similar to those found in many other familiar computer applications. The menu items are briefly explained below:

File.   Use this to print, mail, or save the current document into a file. This menu contains items that let you open a location (go directly to a URL), open a file, or quit the application in order to end the current WWW session.

Edit.   The items in this menu allow you to copy items from the current document to other applications. This menu also contains an item called **Find,** which lets you search the current document for a keyword, a phrase, or a string of letters. This item is particularly useful when searching a long index.

View.   The items in this menu let you find out important information about the current document and allow you to update it in case changes have been made since you first accessed it. By viewing the source version of the current document, you can determine the HTML commands used in its creation. You can also discover when it was last modified. Some large Web sites are constantly being modified. For example, if you have been reading an online newspaper for several minutes or so, you may want to reload a copy of the current document in case any changes have been made since the time you originally loaded it. You can also "refresh" a Web page to its original state. This function is particularly useful if you are filling out an online form and make a mistake.

Go.   Use these items to "go" anywhere on the Web that you have already visited during the current session. Netscape keeps track of the Web pages in the same order in which you visit them. This is called a history list. You may select any page on the history list by clicking on it.

Bookmarks.   Should you come across a Web page that you want to revisit during a subsequent surfing session, you can create what is called a bookmark. A bookmark in Netscape has the same function as a bookmark you place in a book; it marks a spot that you want to find again later. By selecting the **Add Bookmark** item from this menu, the browser will keep a copy of the Web page's title and URL.

Options.   Netscape allows you various options for displaying the content area (the current Web page) and the browser's menu items. For example, some users prefer to hide parts of the browser's menu in order to maximize the content area screen space. There's a separate item for the preferences you must set in order to use email and Usenet news.

Directory.   Directory buttons can be accessed from either the Directory or the Help menus. These buttons contain lists of interesting Web sites according to various categories. **What's New?** updates the latest developments on the Internet. **What's Cool?** contains a list of the coolest sites on the Internet, cool according to the Netscape staff, that is. **Destinations** includes valuable information about Internet directories and tools. **Net Search** is a directory of tools you can use to conduct Internet searches. **People** lists Internet sites that can help you locate the names and email addresses of people using the Internet. And **Software** keeps you abreast of Netscape Navigator software upgrades, including information about how to download the latest versions or plug-ins.

Window.   Use this to open or to go to other Netscape windows.

Help.   If you have any questions about using Netscape Navigator, go to this menu. It includes a link to frequently asked questions (FAQs) about Netscape and a useful handbook containing a tutorial and detailed explanations of the browser's features.

Toolbar

Netscape Navigator has a row of icons that may be displayed just below the menu bar and Web page title. The toolbar may be either displayed or hidden by selecting from the Options menu. The toolbar items may be represented by either an icon or a word or sometimes by both. Icons are meant to be as transparent as possible: for example, a printer illustrates the print function, a little house signifies the homepage, the point of departure for all your Web journeys. Press a toolbar button (click on it with your mouse) and some operation takes place. In some cases, a dialog box pops up if the command has some options or if you need to provide information. The icons for Netscape Navigator are indicated below.

These two buttons help you navigate the Web. Browsers keep a chronological record of all the hyperlinks that you visit during a WWW session. Chances are that at some point you will want to backtrack to a previously visited site. To backtrack, simply click on the **Back** button. Clicking on the **Forward** button will move you to the top of the chronological list or to the last site visited. The same navigational functions are available from the **Go** menu.

This button takes you to your browser's homepage, that is, the page you see when you start up Netscape.

This button reloads the current document. If the document doesn't load completely, is disturbed in some way, or if the source has changed since you last accessed it, you may want to reload it.

If the images or graphics don't automatically appear in the current document and you'd like to see them, click on this button. A setting in the **Options** menu (**Auto Load Images**) controls whether or not images are displayed automatically. To speed the download time of a Web page, you may prefer to read Web pages in a text-only format and ignore the images altogether.

To open or access a location (URL), click on this button and type in the URL in the popup dialog box. Then press the **Go** button immediately adjacent to the dialog box in order to access the site.

Click on this button to print the current document.

Click here to locate a string of letters or one or more words in the current Web page. This function comes in handy when searching a long index.

 Sometimes you may want to stop the loading of a current Web page, such as when downloading takes too long or when you realize that you would prefer to download another page. Click on this button to interrupt downloading.

Location Field

This field contains the URL for the current document displayed on the screen. If you type in a new URL and press ENTER, the word **Location** will change to **Go To** while the browser connects to the new site. As soon as the Web page is fully loaded, the word **Location** reappears.

Content Area or Document Area

Recalling the television analogy referred to earlier, the content area is akin to the screen on a TV set. Changing locations on the Web is similar to changing the channel on the television. Whenever you change locations, the picture on the screen changes. The browser menu is like the TV's control panel or remote control. The contents of a Web page may contain text, images, or both.

Scroll Bar

If the contents of a Web page are too large to fit onto a single screen, a scroll bar will automatically appear. Scroll bars are typically vertical and appear in the right side of the content area. When a Web site is divided into several fields called frames, horizontal scroll bars may appear as well. Clicking on an arrow will scroll the page in that direction: up, down, left, or right.

Status Bar and Progress Bar

The bar that runs along the bottom of the content area contains several kinds of information. On the far left is a key, the security icon. If the key is blue and unbroken, the document you are working with is secure. If the key appears broken in half, the document is not secure. To the right of the key icon is the status bar. The status bar reports important downloading information. For example, if you are downloading a Web page, the status bar will report the percentage of kilobytes being loaded. It will also indicate when all downloading of information onto your computer is finished ("done"). And finally, to the right of the status bar is the progress bar. Similar in function to the status bar, it gives a visual indication of how much of the Web site has been loaded.

During downloading, you should notice that the Netscape logo (the letter N against the night sky in the upper right corner of the screen) becomes animated with falling stars and comets. If the animation stops, the downloading is either momentarily interrupted or has been completed.

Mail Icon

At the bottom on the far right is an envelope, the mail icon. Netscape Navigator features an email function that allows you to send and receive electronic messages if you have already opened an email account (see Chapter 4 for details about email). If a question mark appears to the right of the mail icon, your mail has not been checked. If the question mark turns into an exclamation point, you have received mail. If you use another email program, you may ignore these features.

SURFING TUTORIAL

As you work your way through the tutorial in this book, the icon will indicate that you are supposed to do something: for example, click on a hyperlink, type a URL in the location field, or perhaps choose an item from the menu. Please keep in mind that the tutorial has been carefully sequenced for pedagogical purposes. If you don't follow the directions in the order prescribed here, the screen shots in the book may not correspond to what appears on your computer screen. The different Web sites that you will visit during the tutorial are a tiny sample of the fascinating and useful language resources that are available online. After the tutorial, you will definitely want to go back and do some more exploring on your own. So let's get started.

Homepage

Double click on the Netscape icon to open the browser. When you start your browser, it will automatically open to a preselected homepage. The homepage is the starting point for all your Web surfing. It may be the homepage of your Internet service provider such as your university or college or it may be the Netscape homepage. You may wish to change the homepage selection by resetting your browser's preferences found in the **Options** menu.

Animal Sounds Site

Click on the **Open** icon . A dialog box will appear. Type in the following URL as shown in Figure 2.2.

<http://www.georgetown.edu/cball/animals/animals.html>

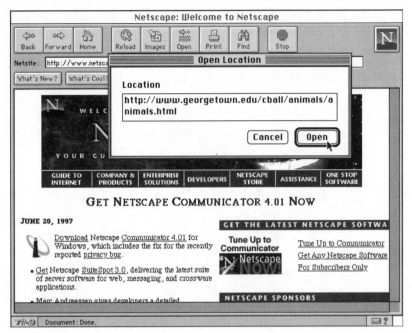

Figure 2.2

Be careful to type all URLs exactly as they are spelled. It is easy to make a mistake since URLs are usually long and contain what appear to be arbitrary strings of letters. Remember, however, that a seemingly small typographical error will make a big difference to your computer.

Click on **Open**. Your browser will connect your computer, called the client, with a computer at Georgetown University, called the server. It may take a few seconds to download the entire page. Notice that the status/progress bars at the bottom of the screen continuously flash information about how much of the page is being downloaded. When the page is finished downloading it should look like Figure 2.3 on page 20.

The page you have accessed is devoted to the linguistic representation of animal sounds. Have you ever wondered how a cow "moos" in Spanish or how a kitten "meows" in Russian or how a bee buzzes in Chinese? Well, this page is the place to go. Catherine Ball, associate professor of Linguistics at Georgetown University and originator of this page, explains its purpose: "Introductory Linguistics textbooks often include a segment on 'onomatopoeia,' with an exercise that involves comparing animal sounds in several languages. This is always a popular exercise: students are fascinated by the cross-linguistic data, and native speakers of different languages can contribute their own data to the discussion."

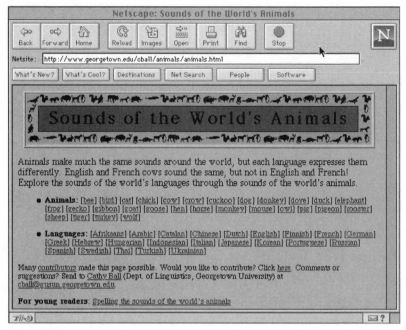

Figure 2.3

Highlighted Links. Scroll down the entire page using the scroll bar on the right side of the screen (but don't click on any links just yet!). Notice how the page is laid out. The first part of the page is devoted to the animal sounds in the various languages. Further down the page you come to a list of related links (sites that are somehow related to this Web page). Next you see information about how you may contribute to this page (it is an ongoing interactive project). And lastly, you find technical information about the page, for example, details about phonetic transcription and how to get the sounds to play correctly.

Scroll back up to the top of the page. Move your cursor over the hyperlinks in the animals list and in the languages list. What happens to the bar at the bottom of the screen as you move your cursor over a hyperlink? The string of letters that you see in the bar is the URL for the link that your cursor touches. And what happens to the cursor itself? Notice how it changes from an arrow to a little hand whenever it encounters a clickable link.

Click on the hyperlink *cat*. Your screen should display a picture of a very cute kitten, as in Figure 2.4. Hyperlinks are color highlighted and underlined so that they stand out from the surrounding text. Play the sound file of the kitten by clicking on the speaker icon and peruse the cat page.

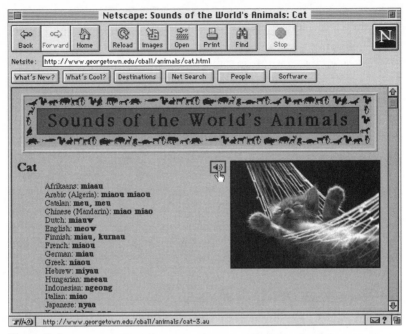

Figure 2.4

WWW Click on the **Back** toolbar button to return to the previous page. You will return to the Web site's homepage. Look at the list of animals. What has happened to the hyperlink *cat*? It has changed color, right? Your browser keeps track of every hyperlink you select and indicates a previously selected link by changing its color. Go ahead and click on several more animals. Remember that you can always click on **Back** to return to the Web site's homepage.

WWW Choose the hyperlink *Spanish* from the language list. Why do so many of the Spanish links indicate that they have already been selected? You haven't clicked on any of these links before, have you? If you are perplexed, click on the link *el gato* and you will figure out the mystery. *El gato* is the Spanish word for cat, and you have already visited the cat page. The computer keeps track of the sites you have already visited and seen even though the names of the links may be different. Just like the expressions "the White House" and "the residence of the First Family" refer to the same location in Washington, D.C., with the same address (1600 Pennsylvania Avenue), the links *el gato* or *cat* refer to the same Web page and therefore share the same URL **<http://www.georgetown.edu/cball/animals/cat.html>**.

WWW Click on an animal link you have not yet explored and make a note of the Spanish word for the animal's sound. Now click on the Spanish link and you will see that the animal you previously selected is now highlighted. Keeping track of hyperlinks is extremely important in a hypertext environment where everything is linked to everything else. It is easy to get lost in cyberspace, and the color coding of previously selected hyperlinks marks your path like a trail of bread crumbs.

Navigation Via Site Options.   Sometimes a well-designed page can keep you from getting lost. Well-designed Web pages usually include built-in navigation buttons to help you find your way around more easily. These navigation buttons are usually found at the top or bottom of the Web page.

Click on a language link (for example, French or Turkish) and scroll down to the bottom of that page. You will notice that the animal and language directories found on the homepage are also found here. This means that you don't always have to go back to the homepage of a site to navigate your way around.

Online Grammars/Dictionaries Site

Now let's explore a more complex Web site devoted to online grammars and dictionaries in over 100 languages.

Click on the URL currently in the location field and type in the new URL:

<http://www.bucknell.edu/%7Erbeard/grammars.html>

Then press your computer's ENTER or RETURN key. This is a different way to open a new URL. Remember that to access the Sounds of the World's Animals page, you selected **Open** from the toolbar and typed in the URL. The online grammar site, shown in Figure 2.5, orginates from a server at Bucknell University and is maintained by Robert Beard, professor of Russian and Linguistics. Professor Beard comments that "this page maintains links with online grammars of as many languages as can be found on the Web. It includes all types of grammars: reference grammars, learning grammars, and historical grammars." The grammar site is linked to a companion dictionary site that includes links to over 300 dictionaries of more than 100 languages.

Understanding URL Syntax.   Scroll down the entire list of grammars. Are there languages here that you have never heard of before? This site is an excellent example of a link list, a master list of related links. These links represent Web sites that exist on servers all over the world. To figure out where a site originates, you need to know a little

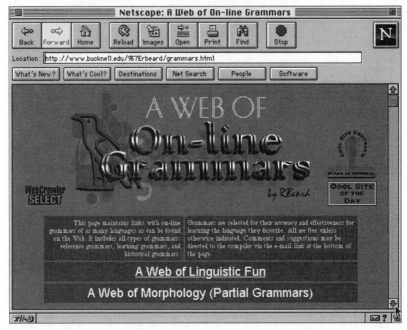

Figure 2.5

about the syntax of a URL. For example, let's take a look at the URL for the online grammar site.

<http://www.bucknell.edu/%7Erbeard/grammars.html>

Breaking down a URL into its component parts is like analyzing or parsing a sentence. To parse a sentence, you must know the parts of speech. Similarly, to parse a URL, you need to know the form, function, and order of its component parts. The first part of the URL (http://) indicates the protocol (the rules governing how computers exchange information with each other). The protocol that is used for transferring Web pages from computer to computer is called "hypertext transfer protocol" (http://).

Other Internet protocols are used to transfer different kinds of information on the Internet. The most well-known protocols and their prefixes are: FTP (ftp://), telnet (telnet://), WAIS (wais://), and Gopher (gopher://). FTP stands for "file transfer protocol" and refers to the set of commands used to transfer files between computers on the Internet, for example, when you wish to download a set of interactive grammar exercises from a Web site. Telnet allows you to log onto another computer from your own computer using a username and a password. WAIS refers to a program that searches a variety of Internet databases by looking for specific keywords in documents rather than simply looking at document titles. The term "Gopher" refers to a program for accessing Internet information through hierarchical menus. Gopher arranges files in a text-only format that is especially useful for library catalogs. And finally, there is a special protocol used to send and receive electronic mail (mailto://). Note that URLs use only double forward slashes (//).

After the protocol, most URLs (but not all) contain the string "www." which explicitly refers to the World Wide Web. Next comes the domain name, the part of the URL that identifies the location of the server computer. By looking at the URL, you can tell that the site originates from Bucknell University. All educational institutions in the United States are indicated by the domain name ".edu". Remember the Sounds of the World's Animals site? It originated from a server at Georgetown University (www.georgetown.edu). Note that a slash separates the domain name from the next part of the URL, the directory path. This last part of the URL refers to the files of a specific Web site that are "housed" on a server on the campus of Bucknell University.

Let's try a little experiment. Delete the directory path part of the URL, that is %7Erbeard/grammars.html. You can do this by dragging your cursor across it then hitting the DELETE key. The URL should now read as follows: <http://www.bucknell.edu/>. Where will this URL take you? Press the ENTER or RETURN key to find out. To return to the On-line Grammars page, simply click on the browser's **Back** button. Of course, colleges and universities are not the only places where Web sites originate. The box below shows you domain names commonly used in the United States for different types of organizations.

Domain Names

DOMAIN	TYPE OF ORGANIZATION
.edu	schools, universities, educational institutions (University of Texas)
.com	commercial sites (for example, St. Martin's Press, Ford Motor Co., Coca-Cola)
.gov	government (U.S.) (for example, State Department, FBI, Internal Revenue Service)
.mil	military (U.S.) (for example, Army, Navy)
.net	networks
.org	nonprofit organizations (for example, PBS, Red Cross, National Public Radio)

Scroll to the German grammars. Move your cursor over the links and read the corresponding URLs. Do you recognize the type of organization where each Web site is located? The Internet Handbook of German Grammar site originates in the United Kingdom as indicated by the ".uk" in the domain name. All countries except the United States have a two-letter code as part of the domain name sequence. The United States represents the default value for Web site addresses and consequently is indicated by the lack of a two-letter country code. The box below gives a partial listing of country codes. If you want exhaustive details about domain names, including all existing country codes, visit the International E-mail accessibility Web site maintained by Olivier Crépin-Leblond at **<http://www.ee.ic.ac.uk /misc/country-codes.html>**. For more information concerning URLs, consult the Web document *Names and Addresses, URIs, URLs, URNs, URCs* at **<http://www.w3.org/pub/WWW/Addressing/Addressing .html>**.

Country Codes for Domain Names

.au	Australia	.de	Germany	.in	India
.be	Belgium	.es	Spain	.it	Italy
.br	Brazil	.fr	France	.jp	Japan
.ca	Canada	.gb/uk	Great Britain	.mx	Mexico

From the foregoing discussion, you can see that URLs are much more than just addresses. In essence, a URL is like a plan for a trip to a far-away place. It contains information about your means of transportation (protocol), your destination (domain name), and your activities when you arrive at your destination (directory path):

means-of-transportation://where-you-want-to-go/what-you-are-going-to-do
   (protocol)   (domain name)   (directory path)

Select at least three grammars to peruse in whatever language(s) interests you. Then scroll to the bottom of the On-line Grammars page and click on the link *On-line Dictionaries* in the far right-hand corner. You should connect to the Web site pictured on page 26.

Scroll down until you come to the Dictionary Index. All the online dictionaries linked to this site are free. Choose a language from the index and compare several dictionaries. You will probably notice that some are more complete or easier to use than others.

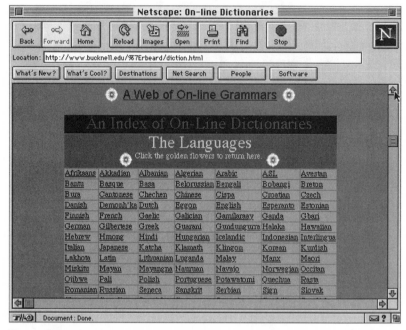

Figure 2.6

Bookmarking.   If you find a dictionary you think would be useful to you in the future, you will want to record, or bookmark, the dictionary's URL so that you can find it again later without having to type in the URL. It is always a good idea to bookmark a site that you find interesting; if you don't, it may take you a while to find it again.

Select a dictionary that you want to bookmark by clicking on the dictionary link. When the dictionary site is fully loaded on your computer, select **Bookmarks** from the menu and click on **Add Bookmarks**. Your browser will automatically record the URL of the dictionary site and will add the dictionary to the bookmark list. To check if the site is bookmarked, select **Bookmarks** and look at the very bottom of the list. The dictionary you selected should be the last item on the list.

Using the History List.   You can also bookmark a site from your browser's history list. Your browser automatically copies the titles and URLs of the sites you visit and displays them in an ordered list. Your browser doesn't keep track of every location you've visited, just the ones you can reach through the **Forward** and **Back** buttons.

From the **Windows** menu select **History.** You will see a list of sites you have already visited during this tutorial. The sites appear in the same order in which you visited them. The most current sites are on the top of the list. When you select a site from the list, the buttons **Add to Bookmarks** (or **Create Bookmarks**) and **Go To** are activated. Select a site from the **History** list and then add it to the bookmarks list. It will automatically be added to the bottom of the bookmark list. Bookmark a few more items from your history list in the same manner.

Setting Up Folders.   If you bookmarked several sites every time you surfed the Web, you would have a long list in no time. To help keep your bookmarks organized, you should use folders. To create folders for your new bookmarks, go to the **Windows** menu and select **Bookmarks**. A popup screen will appear with your bookmarks that should look like this:

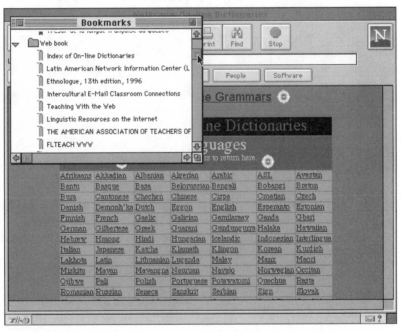

Figure 2.7

Select **Insert Folder** from the **Items** menu. Again, a popup box will appear like the one on page 28. Type your name in the highlighted field at the top, where it reads "New folder."

Click OK. A folder with your name will appear in the bookmarks list. Now, drag all of your bookmarks into the folder. From now on, the browser will keep these bookmarks in your folder—until you decide to delete or change them. If you gather many bookmarks, you will probably want to alphabetize them, which you will have to do manually.

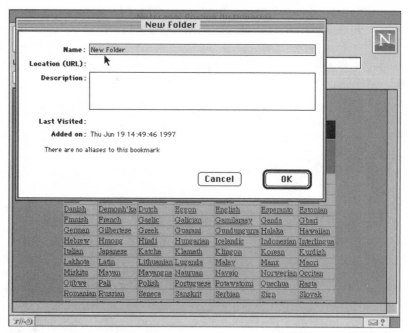

Figure 2.8

Latin American Network Information Center Site

Now let's tackle an even bigger Web site called the Latin American Network Information Center (LANIC). This site originates from its own server and is managed by the Institute of Latin American Studies (ILAS) at the University of Texas at Austin. It is funded by the Andrew W. Mellon Foundation and the Ford Foundation. Ning Lin, technical director for LANIC, states that the "objective of LANIC is to provide Latin American users with access to academic databases and information services throughout the Internet world, and to provide Latin Americanists around the world with access to information on and from Latin America." According to the World Wide Web Consortium, a nonprofit organization that oversees the governance and development of the Web, LANIC ranks as one of the most popular academic sites among all disciplines featured in the Virtual Library, an enormous subject catalog of Web links. The URL for LANIC is:

<http://www.lanic.utexas.edu:80/>

Access the LANIC site by either of the two ways already demonstrated: 1) insert the URL in the location field and press the RETURN or ENTER key or 2) select **Open** from the toolbar and type in the URL in the dialog box.

Figure 2.9

As you can see, the homepage of LANIC is arranged in two different directories—a country directory and a subject directory. Do you know some of the languages spoken in Latin America? Of course, Spanish and Portuguese come readily to mind. But did you know that there are hundreds of indigenous languages also spoken there?

Scroll down to the Subject index and click on the *Languages* link. Some of the links found here are also listed in the On-line Grammars site that you just visited. For example, suppose that while you were visiting the On-line Grammars Web site, you had selected a Quechua (a language spoken in the Andes of South America) grammar. That very same Quechua grammar link would now appear highlighted at the LANIC site. Remember that your browser dutifully records all the links you select until you quit Netscape.

Doing a Keyword Search.   LANIC is a treasure trove of information about Latin America. In fact, you may be a little overwhelmed by the amount of interesting stuff to be found here. Not to worry. Your browser can help you sift through the mountains of information. Suppose you have to give a report on the Ancient Mayan language and culture of Mexico for a Spanish or an Anthropology class; the LANIC site would be an excellent place for you to start your search.

Go back to the LANIC homepage and select the link *Mexico* from the country directory. Suddenly you have more than a hundred links related to Mexico. Instead of reading through all of the links to find those that pertain to your report topic, take a short cut.

Select **Find** from the toolbar. In the dialog box type the keyword *Maya* and click on **Find** as shown below:

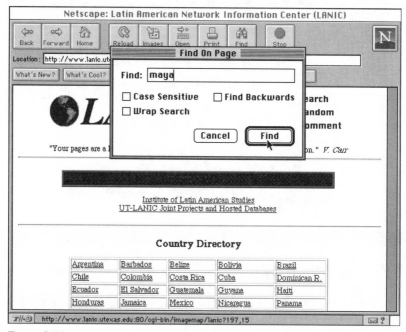

Figure 2.10

The browser automatically seeks out the first occurrence of the word *Maya* beginning at the top of the Web page. To continue your keyword search you can either go back to the **Find** button and click on it again or you can go to the **Edit** menu and select **Find Again**. The browser will signal if there are no more instances of *Maya* on the current Web page. Note that the **Find** command will recognize only the string of letters you enter and nothing else. So you must be careful to choose the most effective word for your search. For example, which keyword will be more effective: *Maya* or *Mayan*?

Type *Mayan* into the **Find** dialog box and then select **Find Again** from the **Edit** menu. You will discover that *Mayan* does not help you find as many links as *Maya* does. Why? What principle about searching indexes can you infer from this brief exercise? Well, there are several principles. First, remember that computers are only as smart as the people who use them. Computers and browsers are *tools* for accessing information, and like all tools, they require an intelligent user for good results. Second, pay attention to prefixes and suffixes. When you type a string of letters into the **Find** dialog box, the computer will search out that string wherever it appears. Consequently, there will be more tokens of *Maya* since it is embedded in the word *Mayan*. On the other hand, the computer will not indicate any instances of *Maya* should you be searching for the string *Mayan*. The point is that prefixes and suffixes limit your search in important ways. However, if you are searching a really big database, you may wish to narrow your search options. You will find out more about conducting Web searches in Chapter 3. For now, let's get back to our project on Ancient Mayan culture and language.

Using Copyrighted Material.   One of the great things about information stored on the Web is how easy it is to copy. And since all the information is in digital form, your computer can copy a photo as easily as it can copy a page of written text. Every text, every sound, every image on the Web can be effortlessly copied as a file onto your computer. Just think how fantastic your report on Mayan culture will look with beautiful color maps and photos from the Web.

Before you start copying material from the Web, however, you should know a little about copyright and intellectual property rights. So first check if the material is copyrighted. Material that is copyrighted will be indicated by the word "copyright," the symbol ©, and the name of the person or organization who holds the copyright. For example, this book's contents on paper and in any electronic form are copyrighted © 1998 by St. Martin's Press. While many Web pages are carefully marked for copyright, some are not. As a good rule of thumb, assume that all material is copyrighted unless you know for a fact that it is not. If you wish to use material under copyright, you must always ask permission. Many Web pages provide the means of contacting the author or editor directly via email.

If you intend only to include the copyrighted material in your report on Ancient Mayan culture and don't intend to exploit it for commercial purposes, then you may use the material according to the "fair use" provisions of the copyright law. Fair use of copyrighted material in educational settings means that you may copy the material as long as you do not infringe on the author's or publisher's benefits. Of course, whenever you copy something from the Web (or from any other source), you must still be careful to document it and to reference it appropriately. (For more information on this topic visit *Online! A Reference Guide to Using Internet Sources* at **<http://www.smpcollege.com/online-4styles~help>**.)

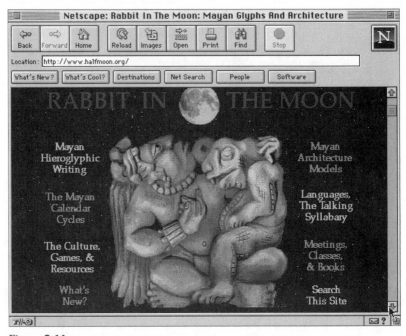 Go back to LANIC's homepage and select the *Languages* link from the subject directory. Scroll down until you come to *Mayan Languages*. Click on *Rabbit in the Moon*.

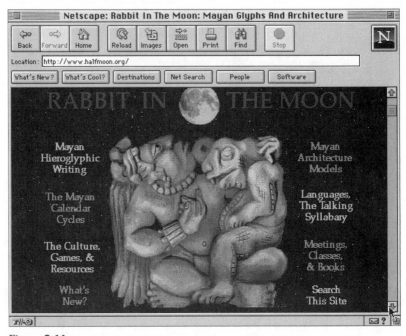

Figure 2.11

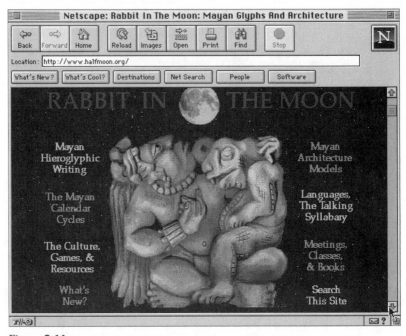 **Saving Text and Source Files.**   Click on the link *Culture, Games, and Resources*. Next, click on the *Culture, Oddities, and Games* link. Finally, click on *Be Attractive the Classic Maya Way* for some ancient beauty tips as shown on the facing page. Make a copy of this Web page so that you can use the information for your report.

 From the **File** menu, select **Save As**. A dialog box will appear with the highlighted words *Classic Mayan Beauty Tips*.

Note that you may save the Web page in two different formats: text file and source (HTML) file. The format options are found below the **Save As** dialog box. Choose a format option by clicking on the arrow, next highlighting either text or source, and then by unclicking. If you save the page as a text file, you will copy the text and nothing else. If you save the page in its source format, you will copy the text as well as the HTML tags or commands that surround the text but not the images. The text file (Figure 2.14) and source file (Figure 2.15) of this page are shown on page 34.

Figure 2.12

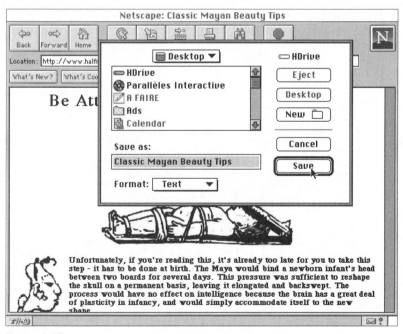

Figure 2.13

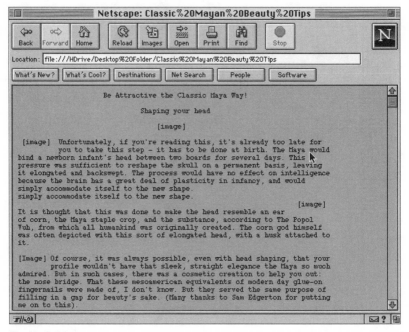

Figure 2.14

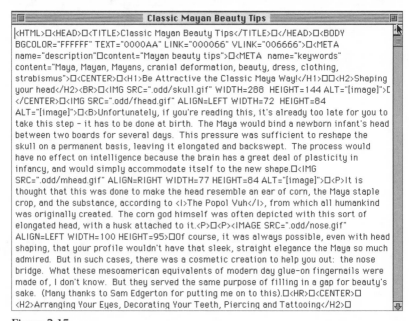

Figure 2.15

For the purposes of your report, you are only interested in the text itself and not in how it is laid out using HTML. So save the page in text format by choosing **Text** from the format options and clicking on the **Save** button. A copy of the page will be saved to your computer desktop. But what about those great images? Wouldn't they look terrific in your report? Well, save them too.

Click on the head shaping image at the top of the page but hold your mouse button down, that is, do not release it. A popup box will appear. Select **Save Image as ...** from the list of options. Next, a dialog box will appear with the highlighted words *skull.gif*.

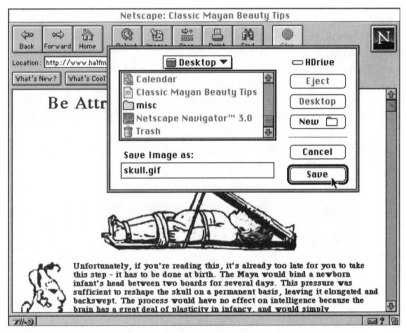

Figure 2.16

Click on **Save** and your computer will automatically save a file of the image and place it on your desktop where you can retrieve it later. If you want to check to see if the image is properly copied, go to the **File** menu and select **Open File**. A dialog box with a list of your computer's desktop files should appear. Scroll down the list until you find the file labeled *skull.gif*, then click **Open**. The Web page's image of a young boy in a head press should appear on your screen. Practice copying some of the images of the traditional headdresses found at the bottom of the page.

CNN Site

The last stop on our surfing tutorial is CNN Interactive, a site that is different than others in several important ways. First, unlike the other three sites that originate from university campuses, it is a commercial site. Second, it is a graphics-intensive site that uses cutting-edge technology. This means that the page contains many photos and images that may slow its download time. Third, this site is constantly being updated and may very likely change while you are visiting it. And last, the CNN site differs from the others in that it is not explicitly about foreign languages and cultures. However, as you shall see, CNN Interactive is an excellent way to stay current about foreign affairs.

Using the Text-Only Option.   Open the following URL: **<http: //www.cnn.com/>**. If you are accessing this site from a modem, you may notice that it takes more time to load than the previous sites. Once it is fully loaded you will understand why. This Web page, shown below, includes many photos and even some animations. Web pages that are so graphically intensive will often allow you to "turn off" all the bells and whistles, an attractive option in case your download time is too slow. Click on the link *Text-Only Version* (upper right corner) to see what the CNN site looks like without the graphics. Then click on **Back** to return to the full graphic version.

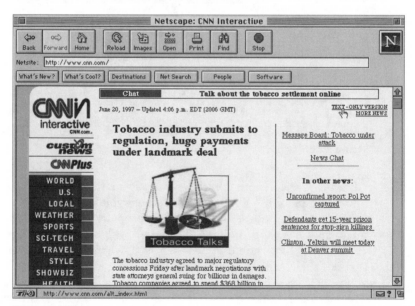

Figure 2.17

Viewing QuickTime Videos.   If a camera icon appears next to an article, it means that there is accompanying video. Simply click the camera icon to download the video. If you don't see any camera icons, scroll down the main index to the *Video Vault* link, which contains many short news and feature videos. Click on any QuickTime video link from the list. As soon as the video is fully loaded on your computer, you will see a photo with a scroll bar underneath. The video is already cued and waiting for you to press the play button. Click on the arrow shown in the screen shot below to view the video.

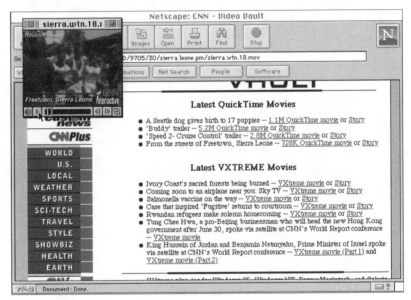

Figure 2.18

Downloading Plug-ins.   Navigator 3.0 includes QuickTime software and as a result can play all QuickTime videos. Sometimes, however, you will discover a sophisticated site that will push your browser beyond its technological limits. In this case, you will need to download some additional software to get your browser up to speed. At the bottom of the CNN page are various software demos and "plug-ins" (software that extends or upgrades your browser). A plug-in is an auxiliary application that can "turbo-charge" your Web browser's capabilities. Shockwave and Java are two popular plug-ins that run multimedia programs on the Internet. For example, you may be surfing along when you happen upon a Web site that requires Shockwave in order for your browser to display that site's pages. In this case, you will need to download and install Shockwave on your computer's hard drive.

Not to worry. Downloading a plug-in is usually free and quite pain-less. Just follow the directions on your screen by pointing and clicking. Of course, you may choose not to download the plug-in, in which case your browser may not be able to read parts of the Web site. If you are interested in downloading something, simply click on the link and follow the directions. It usually takes several minutes to download a plug-in, depending on how much memory it requires.

If you spend more than fifteen minutes at the CNN site, you should probably click on **Reload** from the menu. Netscape will then automatically check to see if any changes have been made to the page since you last accessed it. If there have been changes, Netscape will replace the old page with the new page. When moving around the CNN site, photos will occasionally not load properly. When this hap-pens, you will see a small icon in place of the photo or graphic. Sim-ply click on the **Image** icon from the toolbar to assure that all photos load correctly.

Printing.   From the CNN Interactive homepage, select an article you find interesting. Now click on **Print** from the toolbar. Provided that your printer and computer are properly connected, your printer should print a copy of the page exactly as you see it on your screen, complete with photos or any other graphics: what you see is what you print! Should you want to print only the text portion of the article, save the page as a text file. Do you remember how? Review the steps on page 32. When you have saved the text file to your computer, you can print it out.

Ending the Surfing Session.   To bring your surfing session full cir-cle, select the **Home** button from the toolbar. No matter where you are on the Web, you are always just a click away from home. Clicking on the **Home** button will link you to your browser's homepage, the start-up point for your surf session. Unfortunately, like all good things, it is time for your surfing lesson to come to an end. Click on **File** on the menu bar. Then click on **Exit** from the **File** menu. Your browser will automatically quit and return you to your desktop.

Summary

Let's briefly recap what you learned during the tutorial. First, you became familiar with the major components of a browser such as the menu bar, the toolbar, and the content area. Next, you learned how to open a location by typing in a URL in the **Open** dialog box. Later, you learned that a URL could be typed into the location field to be accessed. At the Sounds of the World's Animals site, you discovered that hyperlinks are underlined and color-coded and change color when selected. At the On-line Grammars and Dictionaries site, you practiced making bookmarks and learned how to use the history list. You also reviewed the basics of URL syntax. Next, you explored the Latin American Network Information Center where you learned how to save files. You also conducted a keyword search on a Web page and picked up a few pointers about copyright and the Internet. And lastly, you visited CNN Interactive, a graphics-intensive site where you practiced downloading plug-ins, viewing QuickTime movies, and printing Web pages. Of course, this tutorial has only scratched the surface of what there is to know about Web surfing. But that's OK. From now on, you should be able to learn by yourself.

On Your Own

The exercises in this section will extend the knowledge you gained during your surfing tutorial—knowledge about the Web and about your Web browser. Use the exercises as a diagnostic test to see which features of your browser you still need to practice. You may need to refer to the tutorial for help.

A. One of the most important things for you to learn is how to help yourself. Life is not a tutorial and someday you have to go it alone. So it's important to know how to find the answers to the inevitable questions that arise when you are surfing. In this exercise, you will learn about using online help and the Navigator's handbook. Start your Web browser.

1. What is your homepage? What is its URL?

2. Go to **Help** menu (your browser may show a question-mark icon in a balloon). Go to **About Netscape Navigator.** What are the plug-ins or software extensions that your browser includes? It is important to be familiar with what your browser can and cannot do.

3. Go to **Help** again and select **Handbook** from the pulldown menu. Many questions about the Web and about your browser will come to you while you are surfing. It is crucial that you familiarize yourself with this online handbook. You don't need to know everything about your browser before you start to use it on your own. But you should know how to ask your browser for help when you encounter trouble. Where in the handbook can you find the:

    ❑ online tutorial?

    ❑ in-depth explanations of each menu item?

    ❑ overview of browser's preference settings?

4. Go to the Handbook's **Tutorial** section. Click on **Learn Netscape.** Are there any topics here that interest you?

5. Go to the Handbook's **Index.** Click on a letter to see how the index is arranged. Is it cross-indexed? Are there links embedded in the index? Why do you think that information is arranged in different ways in the online handbook?

B. Go to Netscape's Homepage at <http://home.netscape.com/>. Scroll down the page until you come to the pulldown menu *Visit a Netscape International Site.* This will take you to the Netscape site in another country (France, Germany, Brazil, Spain, and so on). Choose an international site from the list. You will notice that the international Web page is almost identical to the English site in layout. But look again. This site is not just a translation of the English site. Notice that some of the content is different. How does the international site reflect a particular language audience? In other words, how does it differ from the English site?

C. Go to the World Wide Web Consortium at <http://www.w3.org/>.

1. Click on the link *About the Web.* Scroll down until you find the *Frequently Asked Questions* (FAQ) link. Click on it (<http://www .boutell.com/faq/>). Now bookmark this link for a handy reference. You can refer to this extensive FAQ list whenever you have a question about the Internet or the WWW. By referring to the FAQ list, find the answers to the following questions:

   ❏ What is the W3 Consortium? Where is it located?

   ❏ Can you catch a virus from visiting a Web page?

   ❏ What are HTML and VRML?

2. Go back to the WWW Consortium's page entitled **About the World Wide Web** by choosing it from your history list (go to the **Window** menu and click on **History**). Click on the link for the *World Wide Web Virtual Library.* This is an enormous subject catalog of WWW links. Scroll down to *Languages and Latin American Studies.* Move your cursor over the *Latin American* link. What is the URL? Do you recognize it? Can you parse it? Now click on any subject that interests you.

D. Go to the home page of the **I Can Eat Glass Project** at <http: //hcs.harvard.edu/~igp/glass.html>. This is certainly one of the wackiest language sites on the Web. Begun as a lark at Harvard University, it has grown into a semiserious translation project. Web surfers submit translations of the English sentence: "I can eat glass; it doesn't hurt me." The idea is that your garden variety foreign language phrase book is full of useful though banal expressions like "Where are the toilets?" and "How much does this cost?" Imagine a different kind of phrase book with strange expressions like "I can eat glass and it does me no harm!" The project creator claims that if you were to utter such a thing, you would either be viewed as an insane native or treated with dignity and respect. Either way, you wouldn't be taken for an ordinary tourist!

1. Click on the *Full List* link to get the entire alphabetical list of translations. Can you find a language with translations in several dialects such as Spanish or French? Compare the differences. What is the difference between a translation and a transliteration? Give an example of both.

2. Click on the *Oddities* link on the homepage. How do these "odd" languages differ from the languages on the main list? Who speaks Newfie and Yodaspeak? From what "language" does the following translation come: "Like, you know, I can, like, totally, eat like, glass…"?

E. How about visiting the world's most complete compendium of language facts? The place to go is The Ethnologue, a catalog of more than 6,700 languages spoken in 228 countries. The Ethnologue Name Index lists over 39,000 language names, dialect names, and alternate names. It's perfect for practicing keyword searches of Web pages.

1. Open the URL <http://www.sil.org/ethnologue/ethnologue.html> by typing it in the location field and pressing the ENTER or RETURN key. Scroll down to the *Ethnologue Language Name Index* link. Click it.

2. The index is arranged in alphabetical order with a link for every letter. Click on the letter of a language you are studying or are interested in. When the page is fully loaded, click **Find** on the toolbar and type the name of the language in the dialog box. Does the index list your language? To continue the search, go to **Edit** on the menu bar and click on **Find Again**. How many tokens or occurrences of your keyword appear in the index? Look up several more language names in the same way.

3. The Ethnologue Web site is one of the most complete and up-to-date sources for information about the world's languages. If you want to know who speaks what language and where it is spoken, then this is the site for you. Try to find the answers to these questions:

❑ Which continent has the most languages?

❑ How many different sign languages are there in the world?

❑ What are the major dialects of a foreign language you have studied?

      ❏ In which countries is that language spoken?

      ❏ How many people speak that language?

      ❏ Which languages are historically related to that language?

F. How good are you at interpreting URLs? Can you remember how to parse them? Based on the information provided in the following URLs, guess where the site originates (the country and the organization) and what kind of site it is likely to be. Then visit the Web site to see if you are right.

      <http://www.whitehouse.gov/WH/Welcome.html>

      <http://www.nafta.net/mexbiz/index.html>

      <http://www.repubblica.it/>

      <http://www.kantei.go.jp/index-e.html>

      <http://www.goethe.de/>

      <http://www.paris.org/>

      <http://www.mundivia.es/seleccion/>

      <http://www.state.gov/index.html/>

      <http://www.hrc.org/>

      <http://www.guardian.co.uk/guardian/>

      <http://www.spiegel.de/>

      <http://www.cocacola.com/>

      <http://www.el-nacional.com.mx/>

      <http://www.discovery.com/>

      <http://museoprado.mcu.es/>

      <http://www.riviera.fr/>

      <http://www.lib.utexas.edu/>

      <http://www.loc.gov/>

      <http://www.unitedmedia.com/comics/dilbert/>

      <http://national.gallery.ca/>

G. If you have made it this far you are definitely ready for more advanced surfing lessons. For an interactive surfing tutorial, check out Yahoo! Internet Life's Surf School:

      <http://www3.zdnet.com/yil/filters/surfjump.html>

And don't forget to bookmark the URL for future reference.

3 Searching the Foreign Language Web

In Chapter 2 you visited several language-oriented Web sites where you practiced the basics of navigating the Web and learned how to operate a browser. That brief tutorial probably raised some questions in your mind: Are there other useful and interesting foreign language and culture sites? And if so, how can I find them? Cyberspace is full of interesting foreign language Web sites for you to visit. And relevant sites are coming online every day. In fact, because of the explosive growth of the Web, the real problem is that there is too much of everything—including foreign language sites. Fortunately, with a few tips on how to locate the good stuff, you should be able to find what you are searching for.

In this chapter, you will become acquainted with Web directories (also called guides) and Web search engines, two related tools for finding whatever it is you're looking for on the Web. A directory is a Web site that provides links to other sites arranged according to topic or subject. For example, in Chapter 2 you visited the Latin American Network Information Center (LANIC) of the University of Texas at Austin, a well-known directory of informative links pertaining to Latin America. This directory's value depends on a staff of Latin American experts who review pertinent Web sites and select those that meet certain standards. A good directory should make information more accessible by organizing it into easy-to-understand categories. Remember that the LANIC arranges sites according to country or topic (for example, Languages, Economy, Tourism, and so on).

Before you can use a directory site, however, you must first locate it on the Web. To do that, you'll need a search engine. A search engine is software that conducts keyword searches of a specified database. Do you remember the keyword search you conducted on Mayan culture using Netscape Navigator's **Find** button? A search engine works basically the same way, although on a much bigger scale. Instead of searching a single Web page, a search engine will cull through millions of Web pages. Simply type in the keyword and the search engine sorts through the Web looking for matches. While all search engines look for word matches, some will even look up related concepts or suggest related keywords for subsequent searches. As you will discover, search engines are powerful tools in the hands of a savvy user.

This chapter is organized into three parts. First, you will learn the basics of using a search engine and get an overview of the main features and some valuable tips for improving your search results. Next, you will take a guided tour through several searches using four popular search engines. The goal of this tutorial is to acquaint you with commercial search engines and to teach you what strategies give the best results. Finally, you will practice your newly acquired search techniques and discover which search engines best suit your particular needs and tastes.

FUNDAMENTALS OF SEARCH ENGINES

Search engines are the primary tools for helping you locate information on the Web. Recent years have seen a proliferation of free commercial engines. Like browsers, search engines differ in such details as databases and design but not in their basic function, which is to find information. And they all work in pretty much the same fashion: You type a keyword or phrase into the dialog box and click on a button labeled **Submit** or **Search** (or something similar). The search engine quickly sifts through a database of millions of Web sites looking for matches to your keyword. Search engines usually allow you to select among various options for conducting the search. For example, you can specify which database to search: the entire Web or some other preselected database. You can also customize how the results are to be displayed; perhaps you are interested only in the URL and title of each site, or maybe you would prefer to have a brief description of each site. Some search engines will even provide portions of the text from every site that you located.

You can usually control the engine's method of searching by manipulating the order or punctuation of the words you type into the dialog box. For example, if you type in the words *German language schools*, your search engine may use this phrase in different ways. It may locate sites where the words co-occur in the same paragraph but not necessarily as a phrase. This may or may not produce good results. If you want the engine to locate exact matches of the phrase *German language schools*, then you must surround the phrase with quotation marks: *"German language schools"*. By adding quotation marks, you instruct the engine to treat the phrase as an unbreakable unit. In this way, you treat the entire phrase as a keyword and enhance the likelihood that your engine will locate Web sites of greater relevance.

Most engines allow you to further refine your search by using what are commonly known as Boolean operators, simple words such as *and, and not, or*. For example, if you wanted to find documents about French impressionist painters, you could specify which ones to search for and which ones to exclude from the search by using Boolean operators. If you used the operator *and* to join the keywords, each document located by your search engine would contain all the conjoined keywords: Monet *and* Cézanne *and* Renoir. If, however, you wanted to find documents that included reference to Monet and Cézanne but not Renoir, you could employ the operator *and not*: Monet *and* Cézanne *and not* Renoir. Search techniques will be discussed at greater length during the tutorial, where you will get hands-on practice. For now, it is enough for you to understand that search engines provide ways to customize searches, thereby increasing the chances of finding what you are looking for.

Search results are typically displayed in list form in order of their relevance to the keywords. Most keyword searches produce copious results—a million documents is not unusual. Typically, each screen will display the results in sets of ten, twenty, or sometimes more. You will need to click on the **Next** button to see additional results. And finally, most engines have help buttons that will give you online tips or shortcuts. If you conduct a keyword search of a city, your engine may provide you with shortcuts to other relevant resources such as maps of the city and weather reports of the region.

To make this discussion more concrete we'll take a look at the design of Webcrawler, a popular and easy-to-use commercial search engine. Webcrawler's homepage is shown in Figure 3.1. At the top of the page, a dialog box appears with the keywords *Hotels in Barcelona Spain* typed in. The cursor is ready to click on the **Search** button to begin the search. By clicking on the *options* link just below the Search button, you can select how you want to display your results. A standard feature of all search engines is the **Help** button. Notice that Webcrawler's **Help** button is located in the menu to the left. By clicking on this button, you will receive information about search methods specific to Webcrawler, such as the use of Boolean operators. Notice that the rest of the screen is a directory of preselected sites pertaining

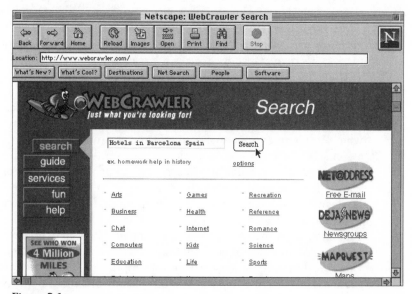

Figure 3.1

to general topics such as Business and Health. If you click on any one of these links you will find a list of pertinent sites that the editors of Webcrawler have selected for their general excellence. In fact, you could click on the *Travel* link to find information about hotel rooms in Barcelona. On the right of the screen are other resources for conducting specific kinds of searches: address searches, map searches, news article searches, and so on. From this single page, you can access an astounding amount of information.

Webcrawler's results of the *Hotels in Barcelona* search are displayed in Figure 3.2. These results are ranked according to their relevance with the most relevant documents appearing first and the least relevant appearing last. Of the 44,555 documents found, the 25 most relevant links are shown here. You can access any Web site appearing in the results list by simply clicking on the link. Note that as part of the search Webcrawler automatically brings to your attention several pertinent resources, such as links to weather reports for Barcelona and the Western Europe Lodging Guide, which are listed in Webcrawler's homepage directory. In other words, Webcrawler combines both a search engine and a directory. In fact, Webcrawler's search engine not only searches the Web, it also searches its very own directory. It is becoming increasingly common for sites to combine a directory and a search engine similar to the Webcrawler site. A site that includes both a search engine and a directory is often referred to as a Web search service or Web search site.

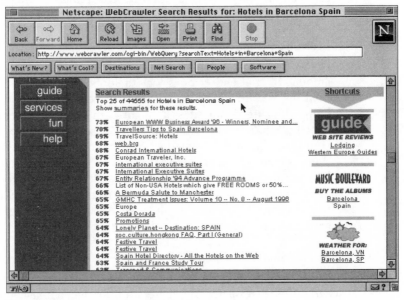

Figure 3.2

TEN TIPS FOR SEARCHES THAT GET RESULTS

Before you begin using search engines, it is important to review some basic techniques for getting good results. Remember that because computers aren't very smart, you have to think for them. And the more thoughtful you are about how you conduct your search, the better your results. By following these simple rules of thumb you should be able to maximize the power and efficiency of your searches.

1. **Use keywords that are descriptive and specific.**

   In general, it pays to be specific when searching for information on the Web. A keyword phrase such as *Spanish culture* is much too broad and will result in literally millions of documents. What exactly are you searching for: a review of Spanish literary masterpieces, some general information about religious holidays in Spain, or perhaps a new recipe for paella? Whenever possible, avoid words that have different meanings in common usage. For example, suppose you wanted to find sites where you could download Internet browsers such as Netscape Navigator and Microsoft Explorer. By all means, don't use *Internet programs* as your keywords; the word *program* has too many meanings. Again, what do you mean by the word program? Are you referring to television programs about the Internet? Do you mean programs of study about the Internet? A better keyword phrase would be *Internet software*, although that too is rather vague. What kind of software applications? An even better, more specific phrase would be *Internet browser*, a specific kind of software for navigating the Internet.

2. **Learn from your results.**

   Remember that searching is not an exact science. A certain amount of trial and error is inevitable. Sometimes your errors hold the keys to future success. Even if your search produces a long list of irrelevant sites, it might turn up a document that contains clues for improving subsequent searches. For example, your list might include one document that is exactly the kind of thing you are looking for. In that case, you would do well to analyze it carefully so that you will know better how to look for more of the same. What is its title? Are there keywords in the text that may be useful? In a nutshell: Always use your results to get better results.

3. **Know when to broaden your search.**

   While it is a good rule of thumb to use specific keywords (*Ferrari* rather than *sports car*), there are times when a keyword will not give the desired results because it is too specific. If this is the case, think of a synonymous but more general term and try again. Suppose the rather specific phrase *Russian verb review* produces poor results. Try again but with a broader keyword phrase like *Russian grammar review* or *Russian grammar tutorial* or *Russian grammar course*. After all, aren't you likely to find a verb lesson within a grammar review?

4. **Check your spelling.**

If you misspell your keyword, you almost certainly will not find what you want. If your keyword is a foreign one, make doubly sure that you have spelled it correctly. Even if you are sure of the spelling, it is easy to make a typographical error. For example, the erroneous keyword *Cattelonia* will get you nowhere if you want information about *Catalonia,* the popular region of Spain's northeastern coast.

5. **Use Web directories in addition to search engines.**

Sometimes the information you want is more easily found by searching a directory or guide than by sifting through the entire contents of the Web with a search engine. The major Web directories employ editorial teams whose job is to evaluate and select the very best Web sites in different subject areas. If you conduct a search and the search engine suggests that you consult the links in a directory, it is usually advice worth taking.

6. **Use foreign language keywords to search for foreign language information.**

If you are looking for the German text of a recently enacted law in Switzerland, chances are that you will find it more efficiently by using a German language search engine and by searching for the law by its German name. In general, if you are looking for a foreign language document, use foreign language keywords and a foreign language search engine to do the job.

7. **Try advanced search techniques when simple keyword searches fail.**

Click on your search engine's **Help** button to see how to conduct more sophisticated searches by using Boolean operators and other advanced techniques. By using advanced search techniques you can specify the words that must and must not appear in documents.

8. **Use the right tool for the right job.**

You wouldn't use a wrench to pound nails, would you? Well, maybe . . . if you didn't have a hammer. But the point is that a hammer is made expressly for pounding nails. While general search engines are suitable for conducting general text searches of the Web, don't overlook specialty tools that conduct searches of the Web for specific kinds of information: for example, photos, email addresses, or city street maps.

9. **Use several different search engines.**

While most search engines work in similar ways, they all draw from slightly different databases. If you are not satisfied with the results that a particular search engine yields, try the same search with a different engine. You don't need to use ten different search engines for every search—that's overkill. But it helps to expand your repertoire in case the search you conduct with your favorite engine leaves you empty-handed.

10. **Consider your search engine's database.**

Why search the entire Web when you know that the pertinent information resides in a specific database or in a specific place on the Web? Let's say that you are looking for the French Ministry of Education, an official governmental agency. Why search the world for a site that you can safely assume resides in France? You would do well to restrict your search to French Web sites. This will speed up your search and increase the possibilities of finding what you are looking for. In other words, before you search, ask yourself which database you should be searching.

WEB SEARCH TUTORIAL

The best way to learn how to conduct searches is simply to conduct them. There is no substitute for hands-on experience. So, let's get started. Remember that this tutorial is carefully structured to aid your learning. If you don't follow the steps of the tutorial, the screen shots in this book may not resemble what appears on your computer screen. Remember that the symbol ![WWW] indicates that you are to do something: Click on a browser button, type in a keyword, and so on.

![WWW] Open Netscape Navigator by double clicking on its icon (this tutorial is based on Navigator version 3.0). Remember that when you open Navigator to begin a Web session, it will automatically access a preselected homepage. If you are accessing the Internet from a university, your screen will most likely show the university's homepage. You should also remember that your browser has various options for displaying what appears on the screen. For the purposes of this lesson, it will be necessary for the toolbar, the location field, and the directory buttons to be visible at all times.

Click and hold the **Options** menu key at the top of your screen. Is there a check beside the words: toolbar, location, and directory buttons? If not, then they have been "turned off" or hidden from view. To make them reappear on your screen, simply move your cursor to the unchecked word and release the mouse. Now select **Options** from the main menu again and you will see that the word is checked. Repeat until all three words have a check.

Netscape Net Search

From the Directory button row, click on the **Net Search** button as in Figure 3.3. Netscape has assembled many of the most powerful and popular search engines currently available. This is an excellent place to start your Web search tutorial. You don't need to bookmark it since it is already a permanent part of your browser. The Netscape Net Search homepage shown in Figure 3.4 contains a lot of information. At the top of the page, notice buttons for four major search engines: Excite, Infoseek, Lycos, and Yahoo!. Each one of these search engines has its own directory.

Scroll down the page to peruse its contents. You should find a section entitled "More Search Services" that includes information about various search engines, Web guides, online yellow pages, and topic-specific resources. Near the bottom of the page you will find two windows side by side; these are popup menus indicated by the down arrows. The one on the left reads "Guide to Internet" and the one on the right, "International Search." Select the International Search menu and choose a for-

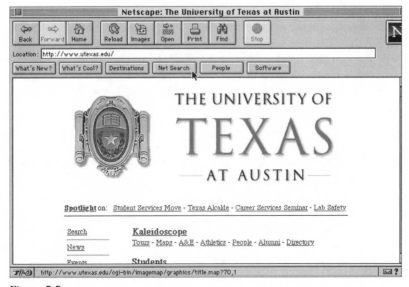

Figure 3.3

Figure 3.4

eign site from the popup list. Now click on **Go**. Take a minute to look over the international page you have selected. Are you surprised to discover that there are so many search engines in that language? Did you know that there are engines that conduct country-specific searches? After you look around, go back to the Netscape Net Search page. Either click on your browser's **Back** button until you arrive there or use the **Go** menu. While the Netscape Net Search page is an excellent resource, a place to do one-stop shopping for search engines, it is also a good idea to visit the homepages for the various search engines because they include services and links not found on Netscape's Net Search page. During the tutorial, you should bookmark each search engine's homepage. Now, let's begin searching the Web.

Excite

First we will visit a popular Web search site called Excite. Remember that a search site combines both a directory and a search engine. In the browser's location field, type in Excite's URL: <**http://www.excite .com/>**. Then press the ENTER or RETURN button on your keyboard. Remember that you can also enter a URL by selecting **Open** from the menu and typing it into the popup window. You can also access the Excite site by clicking on the **Excite** button in the Netscape Search Page. Make a bookmark of the Excite homepage by selecting **Add Bookmark** from the Bookmark menu.

Let's say that you have to do a report on the Catalan language for your Spanish class. Catalan is the language spoken in the Catalonia

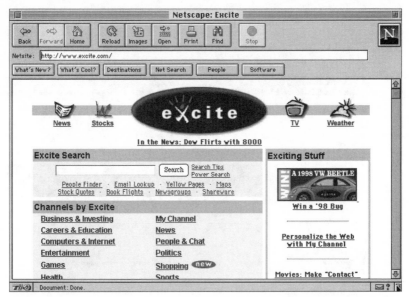

Figure 3.5

region of northeastern Spain. It is a Romance language closely related to both Spanish and French. Let's begin our search by typing in the keyword "Catalan" and clicking on **Search**. It will take Excite a while to locate the relevant documents, so be patient. When the search is completed, Excite will display the results, as shown in Figure 3.6.

Notice that Excite suggests other related keywords that you might try such as "catalonia" and "catalans." Click on *About your results* to display the numerical results of your search. Excite found 8,964 relevant documents when this search was conducted in July 1997. Your search today may indicate a different figure. Note the percentage immediately to the left of each document title. This indicates the degree of relevance of each document as calculated by the search engine's algorithm. The higher the percentage, the more confident you can be that the site listed matches your search query. Excite displays the document's title, its URL, and a brief summary taken from the document's text. You may select other display options, such as *View Titles Only* if you want to reduce the amount of text to read, or *View by Web Site* if you want to see all the relevant pages listed at one Web site. One very helpful feature of the Excite search engine is the *More Like This* link beside every document listed. If you find a document that is just what you are looking for, click on the *More Like This* link and Excite will try to find matching documents.

Scroll down the results list. You will find, among other things, documents referring to Catalan software and Catalan songs. Do you

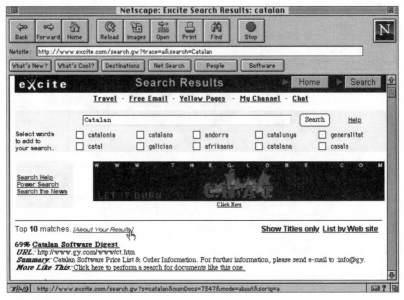

Figure 3.6

recognize the potential weakness in your keyword? You did not specify that you were primarily interested in the Catalan *language*. Nevertheless, there is a document called "Learning Catalan on the Internet." Click on it to see what kind of resource it is. The author or Webmaster of this site describes the document like this: "These pages are meant to be a starting place for people who wish to learn Catalan on the Internet, or those searching for information about the Catalan language. They are primarily aimed at English-speaking people, but speakers of any language will be able to use some of the resources found here." This site is just what you need to get started on your report. As you look at all the various Catalan language links, do you recognize any sites that you visited in Chapter 2?

After you have taken a good look at this very relevant site, you should be thinking about Tip #1 described earlier in this chapter ("Use keywords that are specific and descriptive") and Tip #2 ("Learn from your results"). What can we learn from this site in order to formulate a more explicit keyword? Well, this site is primarily about resources for learning the Catalan language. Why not use those words in a keyword phrase: "Catalan language resources." Excite's technology allows you to search the Web using natural language phrases as keywords. Not only will Excite look for matches to all the keywords in a query phrase but it will also look for concepts and ideas that are closely related to the words in your query. The editors of Excite explain how this search protocol works: "Suppose you enter **elderly people financial concerns** in the query box. In addition to finding sites containing those exact words but not necessarily in that order, the search engine will find sites mentioning the **economic status of retired people** and the **financial concerns of senior citizens**."

Go back to Excite and enter "Catalan language resources" and click on **Search**. Now look at the results list. Do you see any differences? Well, first of all, you have greatly increased your results—over 4 million! That is not necessarily a good thing since you don't have time to sift through 4 million sites, do you? Fortunately, you don't have to. Notice that the relevance scores of the top ten sites have increased and that the sites themselves appear very similar in content; they are all more or less about learning the Catalan language.

In addition to getting information about the Catalan language for your report, you'll need to find out something about the region in Spain where the language is spoken—Catalonia. You may remember that Excite suggested that term as a potentially good keyword. But instead of using Excite again, let's follow Tip #9 ("Use several different search engines") and Tip #10 ("Consider your search engine's database") and use a Spanish search engine this time.

Click on the *Net Search* button from Navigator's **Directory** menu. When the Netscape Net Search page is fully loaded, scroll down the page to the International sites popup box. Select Spanish from the box and click on **Go**. You will arrive at a page entitled "Sistemas de Búsqueda," the Spanish equivalent for "search engines." All of the sites featured on this Web page, shown in Figure 3.7, are Spanish-language

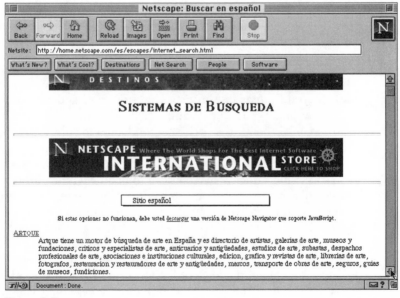

Figure 3.7

search engines and directories. Some engines search the entire Spanish-speaking world (for example, Cibercentro and Olé!) while others
are country or region-specific (Mexico Web Guide). In fact, there is
even a directory devoted exclusively to Catalonia and all things Catalan. Can you find it?

Scroll down to the bottom of the list and click on the *Vilaweb/Cata-
lan Highway* link. Now you have really hit the jackpot. With links to
over 5,000 Catalan-language sites, including the major Barcelona
newspapers and Catalan television and radio stations, Vilaweb is currently the largest Catalan language and culture site on the Internet. In
fact, it is so large and so rich a database of Catalan information that it
comes with its very own search engine! If you don't read Catalan, you
can click the *English* button on the left to get the site's English version. There is even a chat service, which would provide a good forum
for making contact with Catalan speakers (Chapter 4 will tell you
more about how to contact native speakers via chat rooms).

Let's take a moment to reflect on our search so far. Remember
that the search began with the discovery of a single site called "Learning Catalan on the Internet" that eventually led to a megasite like
Vilaweb (see Figure 3.8). From small beginnings come good things.
Using search engines to untangle the Web has an element of sus-
pense—you never know where the search will take you.

AltaVista

Now let's try the same search using a different search engine called
AltaVista. Remember that different search engines have different
search protocols and different databases that invariably produce different results.

Go to AltaVista's homepage by typing in its URL in the location **field:**
<http://www.altavista.digital.com/>. Bookmark this site, then type in
the keyword *Catalan* in AltaVista's keyword field and click on **Search**.

How many relevant documents does it locate? More or fewer
than Excite? When this search was conducted in July 1997, the most
relevant document (that is, the very first document on the list) was
about a Barcelona football team called the Dragons. Not even football
as in soccer but rather as in American football. So much for relevance!
How could this be? Some search engines like Excite are "smart," that
is, they make inferences about what you really mean when you use a
keyword. AltaVista, however, does not make such inferences on its
own. Even so, how could it come up with such an irrelevant site to
the keyword "Catalan"? The Barcelona football site was chosen
because it included the keyword "Catalan" in its Web site title "Catalan sports." Given this apparent limitation, why would you want to
use AltaVista? Because it searches one of the largest databases of any

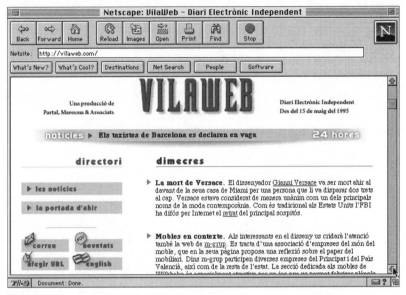

Figure 3.8

search engine. Therefore, it has the potential to conduct extremely powerful searches. But you will need to use it carefully because it will give you *exactly* what you are looking for.

Scroll through the results until you find either the "Learning Catalan on the Internet" site or the "Vilaweb/Catalan Highway" site. How far down the list does it appear? AltaVista's standard option for displaying results is in sets of ten. You may need to click on a number at the bottom of the screen that corresponds to other sets of results. Or you can click on *Next* to go to the next set of results.

Now that we have learned our lesson about AltaVista, let's start over. This time, let's leave Catalonia and try a different search altogether. Let's imagine that you have just read about a new French law that regulates the use of languages other than French in the French media. You are intrigued by the law and want to find a copy of it. Unfortunately, you don't know the law's name. What should you do?

Type in *French language law* and click on **Submit**. You will find the results underwhelming. The sites pertain mostly to the French language but show nothing about law. Remember that AltaVista does not read these keywords as a phrase unless you tell it. Instead, AltaVista searches for these three words separately and tries to find sites where they co-occur but not necessarily as a contiguous string. Try the search again but this time put the phrase in quotation marks (*"French language law"*). Remember that quotes will direct the engine to seek a match for the entire phrase. What are the results now? Unfortunately, they're even worse.

This search obviously calls for some ingenuity. Perhaps you would get better results if you used French keywords recommended in Tip #6 ("Use foreign language keywords for foreign language information") and tried some more advanced search techniques as suggested in Tip #7 ("Try advanced search techniques when simple keyword searches fail"). The French word for law is *loi*, and the French word for language is *langue*. Now specify that the document must include both of the keywords in the document's text. AltaVista's convention for this command is a "+" sign placed before each word. For example, the keyword phrase should look like this: *+loi +langue*. Type in the new French keywords and see what your new bait catches! This time the results should be much better.

In fact, the name of the law you are looking for is likely to appear in the results as shown in Figure 3.9: *La Loi Toubon*. Actually, many of the relevant sites include copies of the law's official text. Unfortunately, French legalese is just as boring and dense to read as English legalese. The law is long and full of arcane legal trivia that is difficult to understand. What you really would like to find are commentaries about the law, preferably written in English. Now that you know the name of the law, you can use that information in subsequent searches, as suggested in Tip #2 ("Learn from your results").

Type in *"Toubon Law"* and click on **Submit**. Remember to use quotation marks since this is a proper name and you want the exact match. This keyword appears in the title of a first document listed (Global Vision International, Inc.) Click on the link. You will find the law is succinctly

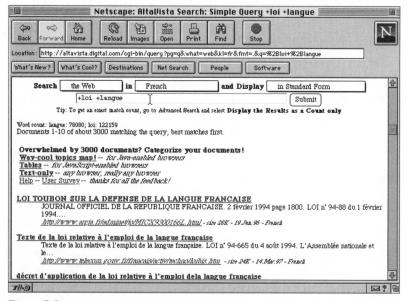

Figure 3.9

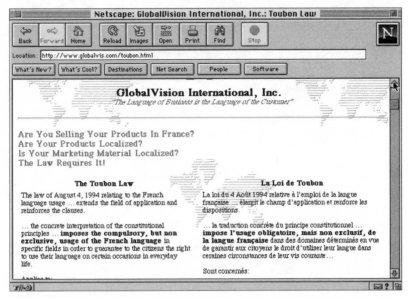

Figure 3.10

summarized in both French and English as in Figure 3.10. There is also information about a recent French court case based on the new language law that involved Georgia Tech. What does it say?

Return to AltaVista's results page and scroll down the list until you find a link entitled *French Studies Web: Law*. You may have to look through four or five sets of results until you find it. Click on the link. This site, shown on page 60, originates from a server in Brigham Young University's main library (can you parse the URL?). It is an excellent resource for French legal documents and includes links to the Library of Congress French legal collection as well as to other online legal documents originating from France.

Lycos

After such a serious topic, you probably need some diversion. How about traveling to an enchanted tropical paradise, say the exotic island of Bali, Indonesia? For our virtual getaway, we will use Lycos, a very user-friendly search site that combines a search engine with a directory.

Type in Lycos's URL in the location field: <http://www.lycos.com/> and bookmark the site when fully loaded as shown in Figure 3.12.

Lycos is one of the best sites to help you organize a dream vacation. You could conduct a keyword search of Bali or of Indonesia. But why bother? Lycos has already done the work for you by locating thousands of informative travel Web sites and arranging them in a way

Figure 3.11

Figure 3.12

that is easy to use. In this instance, you should heed Tip #5 ("Use Web directories in addition to search engines"). Let's visit Lycos's extraordinary travel resources by clicking the *Travel* link in the directory. This will take you to Lycos's travel page as shown in Figure 3.13.

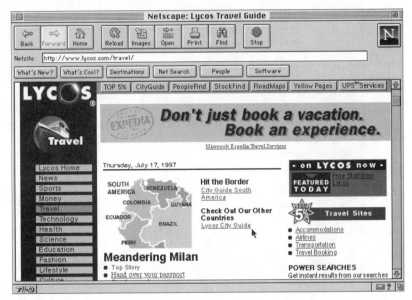

Figure 3.13

Take a few minutes to peruse the information on this page. Updated daily, the Lycos travel page includes articles about the best travel deals currently available, including the best prices on airline tickets and special excursions. Shall we trek through the rainforests of Brazil, backpack across the Alps, or take a hot-air balloon ride over Kenya's famous Serengeti? Oh yes, you were going to Bali, right?

In the middle of the page, you will find a heading that reads "Check Out Our Other Countries." Click on the link *Lycos City Guide* just underneath the heading. "City guide" is somewhat of a misnomer because the link is as much a guide to countries as it is to cities. When the page is fully loaded, you should see a map of the world's continents as in Figure 3.14. Click on Asia (the island of Bali is part of Indonesia, the country north of Australia).

Next you will see the map of Asia. Scroll down until you see the country of Indonesia (the southernmost country in Asia). At the bottom of the page, find the country links and click on *Indonesia*.

The Indonesia page shows the country map and lists the major cities and islands. Can you find Bali on the map? Bali is the first link in the list under the rubric "Islands." Click it to visit Bali!

The Lycos Bali page (Figure 3.15) contains a brief yet informative text for people considering a vacation to Bali. To the right of the text are twenty-five links to excellent Web sites about Bali arranged by categories: Visitor's Guide, Culture and History, News and Weather, and Entertainment. Remember that the Lycos staff has previewed these links and included them here because of their high quality. Imagine how long it would have taken you to find these Web sites by your-

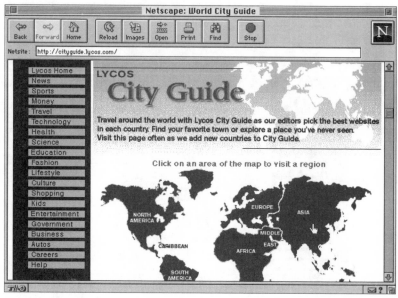

Figure 3.14

Figure 3.15

self! The moral of the story: A good directory can save huge amounts of time when you're looking for information on the Web. Get to know what kinds of information a Web directory typically includes.

Return to Lycos's homepage (*Lycos Home* from the menu). The Lycos site includes several other specific search tools that must be experienced to be believed. At the very top of the page is a yellow menu of specialized searches that includes the CityGuide tool that you just used to visit Bali. To the left of CityGuide is Lycos TOP 5%, a personal guide to the "best" sites on the Web. The Lycos staff decribes the TOP 5% guide as a "selective directory of top-shelf sites rated by the Web's most experienced reviewers." Check it out. You won't be disappointed.

After you have visited the Lycos TOP 5% guide, return to Lycos's home-page and select **Pictures & Sounds** from the menu. This is a specialized search engine that will sort through all the picture and sound files on the Web. Let's try it out. Look for photos of celebrities by typing in their name as the keyword: Princess Diana, Keanu Reeves, Jacques Cousteau, Michael Jordan, Bill Clinton. Or look for photos of interesting places: the Eiffel Tower, Machu Picchu, Tiananmen Square, the Great Pyramids, the Panama Canal, your university, and so on. Can you find a photo of the following: a Lamborghini sports car? A tattoo? An electric guitar? And don't forget about sounds. Have you ever wanted to hear how a particular language sounds? Do you have a favorite popular song? See if there is a sound file of it somewhere on the Web. Just type in the song's name as the keyword. And remember that you can copy any image file and audio file from the Web and save it on your computer.

Yahoo!

Our tour of search engines and directories ends with one of the most famous Web guides of all—Yahoo! In the location field, type in the URL for Yahoo!: <http://www.yahoo.com/> and bookmark it.

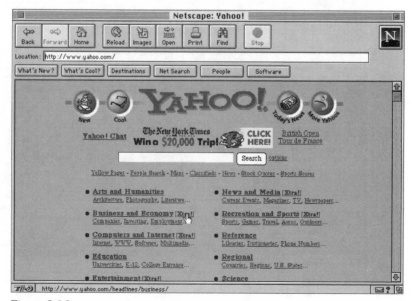

Figure 3.16

The Yahoo! site, like Lycos's, also contains a directory arranged by categories (Figure 3.16). It is also connected to AltaVista in such a way that you can easily surf through the Yahoo! directory then expand your search to the entire Web using AltaVista. Have you ever thought about a summer job overseas? Yahoo! is an excellent tool for finding employment opportunities. When using a directory, the first thing you will need to determine is where to look. Which subject or category should you explore first? Employment is listed as a subcategory of Business and Economy, so let's begin by clicking on *Business and Economy* from the main directory. Next, from the Business and Economy page, click on *Employment*. When you arrive at the Employment page, you will notice that the Jobs category lists over 600 links! That link looks promising. Click on *Jobs*. Notice that Yahoo! helps you keep track of where you are in the directory by showing you all the relevant categories and subcategories at the top of the screen, for example, Top, Business and Economy, Employment, Jobs. From the Jobs list, choose *Seasonal and Summer Employment*. Finally, from this list select the link *Summer Jobs Web*. This site, shown in Figure 3.17 is a searchable database of summer jobs from all over the world. The developers state that most of the summer or seasonal jobs listed in the database are targeted for college students. Let's see if that's true. Where would you like to work? In Europe? Maybe South or Central America? How about Bali?! Simply click in the box labeled "Job search by keyword or location" to fish for a job. By now, you should know how to use a keyword search engine pretty well.

Figure 3.17

TABLE 3.1	A Comparison of Popular Search Engines

EXCITE

- Web search engine and directory
- "Smart" search engine looks for concepts and ideas related to keywords
- Directory categories referred to as channels because design is highly visual

LYCOS

- Web search engine and directory
- Specialized search engines for pictures and sound files
- CityGuides travel information
- TOP 5% index of the Web's best sites according to Lycos editors

YAHOO!

- Most extensive and complete directory on the Web
- Search engine limited to searches of directory
- Links to AltaVista for full-scale Web searches
- Directory organized like an enormous index

ALTAVISTA

- Granddaddy of all search engines
- Largest database of any search engine makes it extremely powerful
- Interprets keywords literally unless instructed to do otherwise
- Requires some knowledge of Boolean operators and other search conventions

You have visited several search sites and have conducted many different searches during this tutorial. Table 3.1 should help you remember the different search sites and their features.

Summary

The Web is a treasure trove of information. At the same time, there is so much information that beginning users typically feel overwhelmed. Knowing how to find things on the Web in the most efficient and effective manner is an important skill that takes time and practice to polish.

In this chapter, you have reviewed the features of two search tools: the search engine and the directory. The search engine retrieves relevant Web documents by looking for matches to the keywords you request. You can control how the engine sorts through the information on the Web by manipulating the engine's database and search methods. In contrast, a Web directory is a menu of topics and subtopics. Which tool to use will depend on the kind of search you wish to conduct and on your personal preferences. Using a search engine is not difficult: Type in your keyword and click on the **Search** button. The hard part, as you have learned, is knowing which keyword will produce the best results. If you are not very clear about what you are looking for, then it is probably a good idea to browse through a directory to narrow your search or to discover a relevant keyword. A keyword that is too broad or too vague will result in an unmanageably long list of hits.

The Web is becoming increasingly international and multi-lingual, an exciting development for students of foreign languages and cultures. One of the sure signs of this new multilingualism is the recent development of foreign language search engines and directories. Moreover, most of the major search engines and directories such as AltaVista and Yahoo! have foreign language versions. If you follow the basic techniques for searching the Web outlined in this chapter and continue to explore foreign language search tools, you should become a master Web searcher in no time.

On Your Own

A. Using the directories of Yahoo! and Excite, find at least two URLs for each of the following:
  ❏ Gothic architecture of Germany
  ❏ Mayan temples
  ❏ Bilingual education
  ❏ Bilingual dictionaries
  ❏ French phonetics lessons
  ❏ Italian wine (Chianti)
  ❏ Spanish embassy in either Canada or the United States
  ❏ World Wide Web guides for beginners

B. Using AltaVista, search the Web for the following keyword phrases, noting the top three items from each search:
  ❏ "Cannes Film Festival"
  ❏ "North American Free Trade Agreement"
  ❏ +recipe +paella

C. Using Lycos, find a brief discussion and graphic for each of the following:
  ❏ International Phonetic Alphabet
  ❏ Paris metro
  ❏ Currency of Bolivia

- ❑ British royal family
- ❑ Pope John Paul II
- ❑ Champagne production
- ❑ Couscous

D. Compare the search engines of Lycos, Excite, and Yahoo! using a keyword of your own choice. How do the results differ? Which engine gave the best results? Which engine do you prefer? Why?

E. Compare the directories of Lycos, Excite, and Yahoo! by looking for the same information in each directory. Are you successful? How do the directories differ? Are they easy to navigate? Do they have the same kinds and amount of information? Which directory do you prefer? Why?

F. You have been assigned a paper about the media of a European country (you choose the country). Find a television site, a radio site, a newspaper site, and a magazine site for the country. Can you find a scholarly article about that country's media? Where would you look for such an article? What keywords would be effective?

G. Go to one of Netscape Net Search's international sites and compare two foreign language directories. Which is better? More powerful? Easier to use?

H. Use any search tool you wish to answer the following questions:
- ❑ Who are Leopold Senghor and Abdou Diouf? What do they have in common?
- ❑ What is the population of Sri Lanka? Of Zaire? Of Peru? Of the USA?
- ❑ Where is the language Tok Pisin spoken?
- ❑ What are the official languages of the United Nations and NATO?
- ❑ What are the names of the radio announcers on National Public Radio?

I. What careers are available for foreign language majors? Use Web directories to locate Web sites on foreign language careers. What careers seem most interesting to you? Are there any careers that you had not thought about before? Try to locate sites that list actual job openings in a career you are interested in. Are there any jobs that look enticing? What are the salaries? Where are the positions?

4 Communicating Online in the Foreign Language

For most people, the ultimate goal of studying a foreign language is to be able to communicate with native speakers. It is an exhilarating experience when you communicate successfully with someone in another language, and it is a motivating experience as well. You're more likely to want to memorize grammar rules and learn new vocabulary when the payoff is real communication. Imagine how much you could improve your language skills and how much first-hand knowledge about the culture you could gain if you corresponded with a foreign Internet pal on a regular basis. Well, there's no need to imagine anymore. Contacting a native speaker has never been easier thanks to the Internet. In fact, there are thousands of native speakers of many different languages who are as interested in corresponding with you as you are with them.

Like many other foreign language learners, you may feel anxious about speaking the language with native speakers. As a consequence, you may shy away from discussions and conversations. Since most communication via the Internet is in written form, however, there is little reason to be anxious. You always have plenty of time to compose or answer a message. In an Internet chat room, for example, you can control your level of participation. Perhaps you want to simply "listen" to the conversation without taking an active role. Or maybe you prefer to dive right in. Either way, you decide. In the not-so-distant future, you will probably be able to talk to native speakers via the Internet in real time, that is, as on a telephone. Until then, the Internet is primarily a way for you to improve your reading and writing skills by sending and receiving electronic messages.

In this chapter, you will learn about the different ways you can contact speakers of other languages via the Internet: personal email, mailing lists, Usenet newsgroups, and chat rooms. You will also learn about the general advantages and disadvantages of these different forms of online communication and how to use them for foreign language learning. And finally, at the end of the chapter, you will perform several hands-on activities.

EMAIL BASICS

Electronic mail, usually referred to simply as email, is the most popular of the Internet's services. The reason for its popularity is simple: convenience. Email is a quick and efficient way to send a message in electronic form anywhere in the world. As long as you have an email account, you can exchange messages with any other email user, making it not only an extremely convenient service but also a powerful one. In the next several sections, you will learn about the basics of email, including an overview of its strengths and weaknesses.

How Email Works

You must have special software to send and receive email, just as you need special browser software to navigate the Web. Commercially produced email programs are available for both PCs and Macintosh computers. Many Web browsers, such as Netscape Navigator, come equipped with email software. Some email programs are free to students and faculty (freeware); others may be downloaded from the Internet for a small fee (shareware). Check with the computer center at your campus or at a reputable computer store for more information about current email programs. You will want to compare options to find the program that best suits your needs. For example, some email programs allow you to send much more than just text; photos and video files are increasingly easy to send via email. With some programs you can even embed Web links in your email message in such a way that the recipient has only to click on the link in order to access the corresponding Web page.

All email software applications share basic functions and by necessity use the same protocols for transferring information on the Internet. Email messages are passed from computer to computer using a protocol called SMTP (simple mail transfer protocol). When you compose a message and send it to a specific address, the message is forwarded by SMTP to your email server, where it is broken down into packets of information that in turn pass through many different computers until reaching the final destination, the addressee's email server. An email server is a computer dedicated to managing the email accounts of many different clients, for example, all the employees at a business or all the students at a college. It's helpful to think of a college's email server as an enormous telephone answering machine that takes messages for many students and faculty. The packets are reassembled in the correct order, and the entire message is kept on the server until the recipient accesses it.

Suppose you want to send a message to a friend in a faraway country. You compose the message, address it, and give your email program the command to send the message to your friend. But what if your friend is asleep and doesn't have the computer turned on? Will he or she still be able to receive your message? Yes, because your message doesn't go directly to a personal computer but goes instead to an email server, where it stays until the recipient checks for mail. Whenever you check to see if you have email, you use another protocol appropriately named post office protocol (POP).

Even though your messages are held for you on an email server used by many other people, only you can access your messages. On some email servers, users share the same space for incoming mail. It is a good idea to check your email regularly and to "clean out" your mailbox by reading and discarding old messages. Deleting unwanted messages frees up more space for everyone. Some email programs automatically save all of your messages unless you manually delete them. Some commercial services automatically delete your unread email messages after a set number of days that you specify in the setup routine. It is easy to accumulate a backlog, especially if you subscribe to various mailing lists whose many members may send you emails.

It is not essential for you to know the technical details of how messages are sent and received in order to use an email program effectively. Instead, what is important for you to understand is that the infrastructure supporting email services is vast and complex, and as a consequence, messages will occasionally get delayed or even lost. Sometimes, if an email message is undeliverable (either the recipient's account is closed or the address is faulty), it will be returned to your mailbox with a brief explanation. For the most part, though, email messages are usually delivered within an hour or two, and often more frequently, wherever the destination—across campus or across the globe.

Opening Your Email Account

Because start-up procedures vary considerably, you must check with your Internet service provider (ISP) before opening an email account. If you are a college student or faculty member, you can probably sign up for email service at your campus computing center. Verify that you have not already paid for email service as part of your student fees. Some ISPs bundle email software with Internet start-up software. At the University of Texas at Austin, for example, students can manage their email using several options. They may choose a free university mailbox service that supports the email program Eudora (Mac or Windows version). Or they may prefer to use the VMS or UNIX mainframe systems, in which case, they can read and manage email directly on those systems. If you are a student, go to the main computing facility on your campus and ask about your email options. After you have opened an email account with your ISP, you must install an email software application on your hard disk and configure your computer according to your ISP's specifications. Now you are ready to begin sending and receiving messages.

Managing Your Email Using Eudora

Despite differences in screen layout, icons, and commands, most email programs share the same basic functions: reading, sending, and deleting electronic messages. The popular program Eudora will be used here to exemplify these basic email functions. Eudora, from Qualcomm, Inc., is a complete freeware email package that handles email using the standard SMTP and POP protocols. Downloadable copies of

Eudora and Eudora plug-ins are available at **<http://www.eudora .com/>**. Eudora gives Mac and PC users access to the same sort of worldwide email services that mainframe users have had for years, but with a much friendlier interface. To start Eudora, double click on the Eudora icon.

Checking for New Messages.   To check for new mail, pull down the **File** menu and select **Check Mail.** Eudora will check for new messages, download your mail, and list all new messages in an **In** window. You will be informed if there is no mail. Whenever you are online (either through a direct or call-up connection) you can have Eudora automatically check for new messages at a regular interval that you set. To automatically check for new messages, open the **Special** menu. Next, select **Settings** (or **Configuration** on older Windows versions of Eudora), then click on the **Checking Mail** icon to change to that submenu. Type a time in the box labeled **Check for mail every. . . .** For example, to have Eudora check for mail every 30 minutes, type 30 in the box.

Reading, Sending, and Deleting Messages.   To read a message, simply double click on it. The message will open and appear on the screen. To send a new message, select **New Message** from the **Message** menu. In the new window, as shown in Figure 4.1, type the recipient's address in the *To* field, and a subject line in the *Subject* field. You can use the tab key or your mouse to move the cursor to any of the fields (e.g., *To:* or *Cc:*) to begin typing. If you want to send copies of the message to others, enter their addresses in the *Cc* or *Bcc* fields. Now press the tab key (or position the mouse and click) until the cursor is in the message area below the dotted line. Type your message. When you are finished, click the **Send** button. Eudora will report the message's progress.

   To delete a message, highlight it. Next, select **Delete** from the **Message** menu. The message will be moved to your **Trash** and will remain there until you empty it (or retrieve the message).

Creating New Mailbox Folders.   Some mailing lists (groups of people who communicate about a particular topic via email) are extremely active and can generate enormous quantities of email. Depending on how many lists you subscribe to and how much email you receive, you may want to create several mailboxes or folders to presort your incoming mail. For example, if you subscribe to a list devoted to international travel and another devoted to international employment opportunities, you could organize your messages by creating new folders for both groups and reserve your original mailbox for general email. To create a new mailbox folder, choose **Mailboxes** from the **Window** menu, click the **New** button, and enter a name when prompted. In older Windows

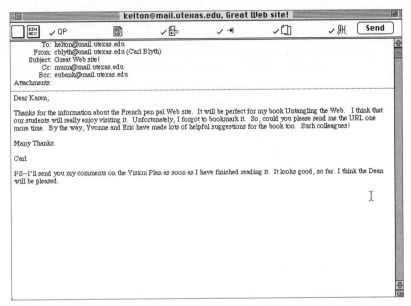

Figure 4.1

versions of Eudora, select **New** from the **Mailbox** menu and enter a name when prompted. All mailbox folders are listed under the **Mailbox** menu, which you can use to change the mailbox folder you are reading from. To move a message from one mailbox to another, highlight the message. Then from the **Transfer** menu, select the destination mailbox where you want to place the message.

The above discussion is a brief overview of Eudora's most basic functions. If you have further questions about Eudora, check out the FAQ file at Eudora's Web site. You may also download a complete user's manual there.

Email Addresses

Before you begin using your email service, you should know a few things about email addresses. It is also useful to know how to parse an email address and to find an address should you lose one, or should you wonder if someone whom you'd like to contact has one.

Parsing an Email Address.   An email address can be divided into its parts in a similar fashion to a URL. Email addresses have three basic parts: the user's local address or name, the *at* sign ("@"), and the domain name. Given what you already know about URL syntax, can you parse the following email address?

<jdoe@mail.utexas.edu>

The first part ("jdoe") stands for the user's name (John Doe). It is customary for people to use their initials or parts of their first and last names written together. Email addresses do not permit blank spaces. As a consequence, if a user wants to spell out his or her name in the address, they must underline the empty space (John_Doe). The word "mail" in the address refers to a server located on the campus of the University of Texas at Austin ("utexas") that is dedicated to managing email. You should remember from the discussion of URLs in Chapter 2 that "edu" indicates an educational institution. Here's another example of an email address:

<modlang@smpcollege.com>

The first part ("modlang") is an abbreviated form of the user's title (Modern Language Editor). The server is located at the College Division of St. Martin's Press (smpcollege). The ".com" at the end indicates a commercial enterprise, in this case, a publishing company.

Finding an Email Address.   What happens when you don't have a person's address or you've lost or forgotten it? You could call or write them a letter requesting their address. As a general principle, however, the best place to find Internet information is on the Internet. If the person is a college student or faculty member, go to the homepage of his or her institution, where you are likely to find a directory that includes current email addresses. Don't be surprised though if you cannot gain access to this information. Some institutions consider email addresses private information and make them available only to their members.

Another way to locate an address is to look it up using a search engine or directory. Many of the popular search engines can conduct specialized searches of email databases. The number of email users is growing so rapidly that email databases are by definition incomplete and in need of constant updating. Since different search engines draw from different databases, your best bet is to try as many engines as possible. Most email databases are cross-indexed with databases of street addresses and telephone numbers. Searches for street addresses and telephone numbers are usually much more reliable since these databases have been in existence longer and are more stable. Here is a URL list of some of the best search tools currently available for searching the Internet for personal addresses (email address, street address, telephone number):

American Directory Assistance: People Search

<http://www.lookupusa.com/lookupusa/adp/peopsrch.htm>

BigFoot

> <http://www.bigfoot.com>

Master Phonebook Server

> <gopher://gopher.nd.edu./11/Non-Notre%20Dame%20
> Information%20Sources/Phone%20Books--Other%20
> Institutions>

Four11 Directory Services

> <http://www.four11.com>

InfoSpace AccuMail Search

> <http://accumail.com>

Internet Address Finder

> <http://www.iaf.net>

InterNIC Netfind Gateway

> <gopher://ds0.internic.net:4320/Inetfind>

LinkStar

> <http://www.linkstar.com>

Switchboard: Find a Person

> <http://switchboard.com>

WhoWhere? Email Search

> <http://www.whowhere.com>

Yahoo People Search: Email

> <http://www.yahoo.com/search/people/email.html>

Advantages and Disadvantages of Using Email

While email has many assets, it also has its share of liabilities. You should be forewarned about possible problems before you begin using it. In general, being aware of both the advantages and disadvantages of email will make you a better user of this powerful Internet service.

Advantages

1. Email is fast. Messages typically reach their destination in only a few hours, sometimes within a few minutes.

2. Email is cheap. At the post office, the price of sending a letter depends on how far the letter must travel, how much it weighs,

and how fast it must reach its destination depending on the class of delivery (Express mail? Priority mail? First class?). For email, none of these factors matter, since all messages are delivered the same way, in roughly the same amount of time.

3. Email is convenient. An email message can be opened and read at any time. No more intrusive phone calls and no more telephone tag. Furthermore, because most email programs support basic word processing functions, you can simply paste your reply into the body of a message and return it to the sender. And unlike a phone call, you may retain a copy of every email message sent or received.

4. Email is for more than just messages. You can attach longer documents (term papers or reports) to the body of an email message. Some programs allow you to attach photos and video files too.

Disadvantages

1. Email is not private (or not as private as you may think). Given that all email messages pass through many different computers before finding their final destination, there is always the possibility that they may get lost, or worse, intercepted. Remember that email messages can be copied and instantly forwarded to other users (literally thousands of users at once). The power of email to disseminate information is a double-edged sword and should give you pause. Before sending any message, ask yourself if the message you are about to send contains information that could be damaging or incriminating should the wrong person see it. Discretion is still the best security system.

2. Email can be forged. Although it is extremely rare, forged emails do exist. You may want to verify the sender of any email containing particularly important or sensitive information.

3. Exceptionally talented writing aside, email is usually not conducive to expressing the nuances of feeling. When you listen to your friends speak, their voices contain clues that help you interpret their emotional state and thus their meaning. Are they being sarcastic? Are they serious? Are they sad? To decide, listeners pay attention to the changes in pitch, rhythm, and intonation of a speaker's voice. Communicating emotional nuance is one area where the telephone tends to beat email. Therefore, when you compose an email message, be aware of the potential for misinterpretation. Otherwise, your joke may come across as a threat. To help communicate emotional meaning, online writers

have developed a repertoire of signs called emoticons, small facial expressions made from typographical characters. Here is a short list of some of the most popular emoticons and the associated emotions:

:-)	happiness	:-(	sadness
;-)	complicity	};->	anger
;-/	skepticism	:-0	surprise

4. Email can be time-consuming to manage. Like many "labor-saving devices," email can eat up a lot of your free time if you are not careful. Every message that arrives in your mailbox, however trivial, requires some action on your part. It is common for people who have not checked their email in a while to find their mailbox jammed with messages. You should also be careful not to join too many mailing lists. Before joining a list, find out how many emails you are likely to receive as a member.

PEN PAL WEB SITES

The growth of the Internet has facilitated a new movement: electronic pen pal services. As more adults begin to discover the pleasures of cross-cultural communication, more and more pen pal services spring up. Most pen pal Web sites consist of nothing more than a database of potential pen pals grouped according to various criteria: age, sex, languages spoken, hobbies. Some pen pal services include brief autobiographical sketches similar to those found in personal ads in the classified sections of a newspaper. Pen pal Web sites vary enormously in size and quality. Large commercially supported sites normally include searchable databases of several thousand pen pals updated on a regular basis. On the other end of the spectrum are Web sites created by individuals who are seeking to build a network of email friends.

While these Web sites facilitate communication with native speakers by making it easier to find a potential correspondent, you must still take the first step. If you find an individual with whom you would like to correspond, you will need to send him or her an introductory message using Eudora or some other email program. In your message, be sure to include how you found out about the person and why you want to correspond. What follows is a sample of four pen pal Web sites. It is by no means an exhaustive list. These sites are discussed here to give you an idea about what to expect from these services. There are many pen pal sites on the Web that you can find by conducting a keyword search (keywords: *pen pal, pen friend, international correspondence, email pals, email networks, email discussion groups*).

Europa Pages Site

<http://www.europa-pages.co.uk/index.html>

The Europa Pages, a commercial Web site originating in England, provides up-to-date information on hundreds of language schools around Europe as well as foreign language materials. It also includes a free pen pal service with a database of addresses of pen pals from all over the world (not just Europe). Each name on the list pictured below is accompanied by a brief personal description including nationality and email address. Since the Europa Pages Web site is dedicated to language learning, most of the pen pals listed in the database are actively seeking to practice their foreign language skills.

To add your entry to the list, just fill out the information form and include a little paragraph about yourself: who you are, what your interests are, and with whom you would like to correspond. Next, press **Send.** Click your browser's **Reload** button to see your personal fiche instantly added to the list. An entry may remain posted for a month before it is removed, at which time you must repost it. Before submitting your entry, you should read through the list of people to see if there isn't already someone to whom you would like to write. You should also be aware that the editors of the Europa Pages Web site forbid any adult-oriented material as well as multiple entries. Moreover, Europa Pages reserves the right to remove any entry deemed unsuitable.

Figure 4.2

FranceWorld Site

<http://www.franceworld.com/sommaire.html>

FranceWorld is a nonprofit service created in 1992 to bring French students in contact with their foreign counterparts. The service consists of two series of fiches: one for students currently matriculated in a French school (elementary through university), another for non-French students. If you would like to post your name, simply click on the link *Remplissez* and fill out the online form according to the directions. All information must be entered for your form to be accepted. By clicking on the link *Cherchez* at the top of the page, you will gain access to the database of French pen pals (see Figure 4.3).

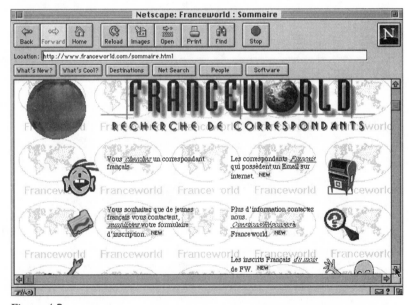

Figure 4.3

Not only is FranceWorld's database of French-speaking pen pals one of the largest in the world (over 5,000 names), it is also searchable according to various criteria, including age, sex, and region of the country. Each fiche is written in simple French and lists important personal information including leisure-time activities *(Loisirs et Sports)*. For example, on Frédéric Meunier's fiche (Figure 4.4), you discover that he is a twenty-year-old university student majoring in languages who likes track, basketball, and music, and who wants to correspond with Americans.

Figure 4.4

The Web of Culture Site

<http://www.worldculture.com/index.html>

The Web of Culture site is devoted to cross-cultural communication and holds much potential for foreign language students. On its home-page you will find several links for contacting speakers of foreign lan-guages. *Travelers*, near the bottom of the homepage, is the link for an interesting list of potential pen pals. Almost all the people listed in this section are adults seeking correspondents who want to discuss interna-tional travel in some form—either past adventures or future trips. The list includes people from all over the world and from all walks of life. The Web of Culture site also features a link entitled *Amigos de Email* whose exclusive goal is to facilitate language learning via email corre-spondence. This list includes the email addresses of language educators seeking email friends for their students. While most of the list is dedi-cated to American teachers seeking foreign student pen pals, a few for-eign teachers are looking for American correspondents.

Another way of making an international connection is by post-ing something on the site's bulletin board service. Click on the link *Visit Our Bulletin Board* and leave a message along with your email address. Your posting and any responses will be listed for all visitors to read. And finally, click on the link *Contacts* for a list of names and

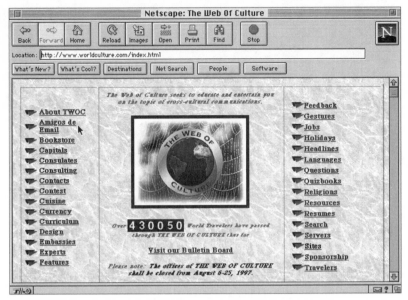

Figure 4.5

email addresses of people you can email for information about their country or language (see Figure 4.5). Note that the list is alphabetized by country and not by name. For example, Henry Yu (China) appears before A. M. Attia (Egypt). If you still can't find a correspondent from a particular country, try contacting the cultural attache of that country's embassy. A complete list of foreign embassies is available by clicking on the link *Embassies.*

St. Olaf's Intercultural E-Mail Classroom Connections Site

<http://www.stolaf.edu/network/iecc/>

The Intercultural E-mail Classroom Connections Site (IECC), provided by St. Olaf College in Northfield, Minnesota, is made up of four electronic mailing lists. Unlike the other pen pal sites that exist to help individuals make contact with other individuals, IECC is aimed at classroom teachers looking for partner classrooms for international or multilingual email exchanges. The IECC homepage (see Figure 4.6) has several valuable links. *How to Subscribe* provides information about how you can become part of one of the IECC mailing lists. You may subscribe to any (or all) of the IECC's lists for free. After subscribing, you will receive a short welcome message explaining how to make your own posting to the IECC mailing lists. The *Related Resources* link

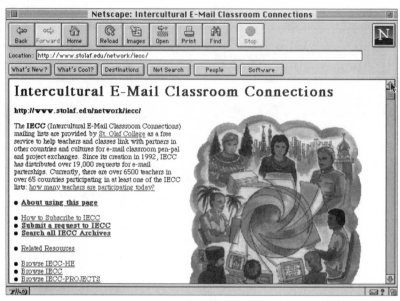

Figure 4.6

contains information about other groups with international email projects. The *Announcements* link is the place to find information about conferences concerning technology and intercultural education. Soon you will be able to download a copy of *Navigating the E-Mail Interculture*, a textbook developed at St. Olaf for teaching students about cross-cultural email exchanges. Finally, there are links for posting your request or for conducting a search of IECC's archives. Even if you are not a teacher, browse through some of the descriptions of the inventive email projects undertaken by language teachers. You will begin to understand why foreign language educators believe that the Internet holds great potential for language and culture education.

MAILING LISTS

If you are too shy to begin a one-on-one correspondence via email, you should consider joining a foreign language mailing list. By subscribing to a mailing list, you can participate in an ongoing discussion in a foreign language about a topic that interests you. A mailing list, also commonly referred to as a listserv, an email discussion group, or an email discussion list, is a group of people who exchange email about a subject that interests them. Any subject is fair game for a mailing list. According to Liszt, a commercial Web site that includes the largest database of mailing lists on the Internet, there are currently more than 71,000 mailing lists in operation (as of fall 1997).

How a Mailing List Works

A mailing list differs from an email pen pal exchange in several important ways. Instead of corresponding with an individual, you correspond with a group. Even if you don't feel like writing messages to anyone, you can still continue to receive messages from all the other members of the group. In fact, you probably should refrain from sending any messages to the group until you have followed the discussion long enough to get a feel for its tone and level. The word "lurking" is used to describe group members who only read messages. While the term seems to have a negative connotation, lurking is completely acceptable behavior in a mailing list.

Another major difference between corresponding with a pen pal and corresponding with members of a mailing list is that the topic of discussion is usually fairly restricted in a discussion group. In fact, you will be swiftly reprimanded if you start sending messages that are considered off the topic. For instance, there are many different mailing lists devoted to sports. If you want to discuss cycling, join a cycling mailing list. If downhill ski racing is your passion, join a skiing list. Just don't send messages about cycling to the skiing list or skiing messages to the cycling list. That would be bad form. And by all means, never send messages to the list that could be construed as an advertisement. Such inappropriate behavior merits dismissal from a mailing list.

Mailing lists are incredibly diverse. Some have thousands of members while others comprise a small network of friends. Some lists are public and welcome new members while others are private and closed to outsiders. You cannot always tell the type of mailing list from the title. For instance, a mailing list entitled "Chain Gang" may be the name of a private motorcycle group. Or it may be a humorous name for a group of cycling enthusiasts who welcome anyone willing to share their interest in the sport of cycling. The main point to remember about mailing lists is that they represent groups—public or private—who often have their own rules and a strong sense of community. As a newcomer, you will want to be polite when first entering their turf. In particular, you should pay close attention to the rules of netiquette, a term derived from the words *Net* and *etiquette*. Netiquette generally refers to the conventionalized "rhetorical courtesies" observed by online writers. For example, netiquette dictates that you write messages that are succinct and pertinent. If you wish to emphasize a word, you should surround it with *asterisks* rather than capitalize it. Words written in all capital letters are the Internet equivalent of SHOUTING.

And finally, mailing lists may differ according to whether they are moderated or not. In an unmoderated list, a message sent by an individual member is immediately made public by being broadcast to the entire group via email. In a moderated list, all messages are evaluated by a moderator before being forwarded to the group's members.

How to Join a Mailing List

To join a list you need to send a special email message to the list's *administrative address*. Most lists are managed by software (the three most common mailing list software are Listserv, Listproc, and Majordomo). The subscription email message typically contains the word *subscribe* and possibly your full name (first name, last name) and the name of the mailing list. Soon after sending your subscription email (a day or two on the average), you should receive a response welcoming you to the list. Save this message! It contains important information including the *list address*, the email address you will use to send messages to the group. It is very easy to confuse the *list address* with the *administrative address*. Remember that the administrative address is only for functions pertaining to the management of the list, such as subscribing or unsubscribing (leaving) the list. The list address, on the other hand, is for sending messages to the group. If you confuse the two addresses, you will probably receive a correction from either the mailing list software or from another member of the list. Here are step-by-step examples of how to join four different foreign language mailing lists.

List Name:	**CHANTER-LISTE**
Description:	An excellent source of information for fans of French music. Discussion is typically in either French or English. You may subscribe to three separate discussion lists:
	chanter-liste: for fans of all French singers/groups
	chanteur-liste: for fans of male French singers
	chanteuse-liste: for fans of female French singers
Administrative address:	**<MAJORDOMO@WIMSEY.COM>**
To join:	Send subscription message to administrative address consisting of only one line:
	subscribe /listname/ /your name/
	example: **<subscribe chanteur-liste John Doe>**

List name:	**MEXICO-L**
Description:	A discussion group for Mexicans and lovers of Mexico about the people, places, and culture of Mexico. Discussion primarily in Spanish but English is permitted.
Administrative address:	**<LISTSERV@TECMTYVM.BITNET>**
To join:	Send subscription message to administrative address consisting of only one line:

    subscribe /listname/ /your name/

    example: **<subscribe MEXICO-L John Doe>**

List name:	**SALSA**
Description:	A forum for the scientific and cultural integration of Caribbean countries. Discussion primarily in Spanish but French and English permitted.
Administrative address:	**<LISTSERV@CONICIT.VE>**
To join:	Send subscription message to administrative address consisting of only one line:

    subscribe /listname/ /your name/

    example: **<subscribe SALSA John Doe>**

List name:	**9NOV89-L**
Description:	A German language mailing list devoted to the discussion of contemporary German politics, in particular the reunification of East and West Germany and the events of the Berlin Wall.
Administrative address:	**<LISTSERV@DB0TUI11.BITNET>**
To join:	Send subscription message to administrative address consisting of only one line:

    subscribe /listname/ /your name/

    example: **<subscribe 9NOV89-L John Doe>**

How to Find Mailing List Addresses

If you think you'd like to follow a foreign language discussion via email, your next step is to find a mailing list that interests you. To help with your search, use the tools you learned about in Chapter 3, namely search engines and directories. However, since you are looking for very specific information, you will need to use specialized tools.

Liszt Site.   Just like the search engines that look only for email addresses, there are also specific mailing list search engines. One of the best is called Liszt. The URL for Liszt is **<http://www.liszt.com/>**.

Liszt is an enormous and regularly updated database of the Internet's mailing lists. Because mailing lists are dynamic communities that come and go rapidly, Liszt periodically contacts them to request information about their status. Like most search engines, Liszt also includes a directory of the best and most active mailing lists. Liszt's search engine works like most keyword engines: Type in your keyword and click on **Go**. Liszt will quickly list the addresses of all pertinent discussion groups in the database. For example, a keyword search conducted in August 1997 using the phrase *French music* (as shown in Figure 4.7) resulted in a single mailing list discussed earlier: **chanter-liste.** Of course, when a more general keyword such as *French* was used, thirty five mailing lists were found (see Figure 4.8). Liszt not only selects relevant mailing lists, it also color codes them according to how much information is available. A mailing list highlighted with green indicates

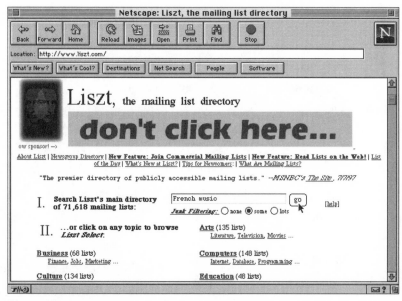

Figure 4.7

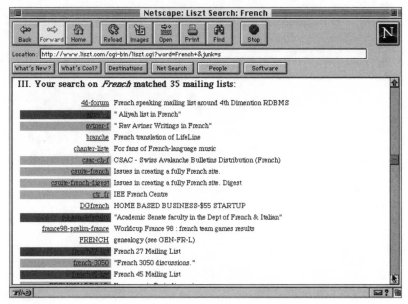

Figure 4.8

that detailed information is available and that the list is currently active. In other words, green means go. Yellow suggests that caution is in order since there is only partial information available about the group. Red means stop: The last time Liszt requested information about this group, there was none available. And white means that Liszt has not yet contacted the mailing list to request information. Besides a search engine and directory, Liszt includes lots of useful information about finding and using mailing lists. In particular, you should check out the links *Tips for Newcomers* and *What Are Mailing Lists?*

Yamada Language Guides Site.   You should remember from Chapter 3 that directories can be even better tools than search engines for locating information, especially if the directory is relatively complete and up-to-date. One of the best places to look for foreign language mailing lists is the Yamada Language Guides Web site at **<http:// babel.uoregon.edu/yamada/guides.html>**. This excellent site has information on over 115 languages and includes an extensive directory of mailing lists in over 50 different languages—from Afrikaans to Yoruba (see Figure 4.9). There are so many discussion groups listed for Arabic, Chinese, French, and Spanish that they have been categorized by region and country. Essential information for each mailing list is available: list name, description, administrative address, and directions on how to subscribe. The Yamada Language Guides directory also includes mailing lists devoted to the fields of foreign language education,

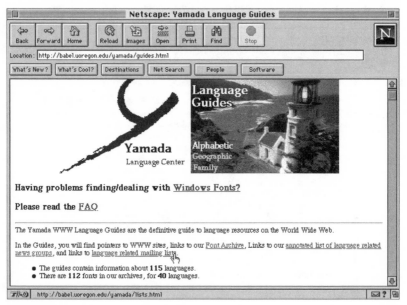

Figure 4.9

translation, interpreting, and linguistics. Eavesdropping on a discussion of foreign language professionals is a fascinating way for you to get a better sense of what these fields are all about.

USENET NEWSGROUPS

Usenet newsgroups, also called Netnews or simply newsgroups, are yet another way to communicate with speakers of other languages. Usenet newsgroups are similar to mailing lists in that they are organized by topic. There are groups for discussing computers, politics, television programs, personal finances, New Age philosophies, Madonna's sex life, and just about any topic you can imagine (and some topics that you'd never imagine even if you tried). Usenet groups differ from mailing lists in several important ways, however. Usenet communication does not require an email program like Eudora but rather a special software called a newsreader (Netscape Navigator and Microsoft Internet Explorer both include a newsreader as part of the browser). In other words, Usenet messages are not exchanged via email to members of a group but are posted by an individual on a site for anyone to read (anyone who has a newsreader, that is). People read and post messages referred to as "articles," which are arranged automatically into categories called newsgroups. These newsgroups reside on servers throughout the world. Unlike mailing lists, which are restricted to subscribed members, any article you post can be viewed worldwide by anybody with a newsreader.

How Usenet Articles Are Organized

As soon as an article is posted, another reader typically responds by posting a follow-up article. And then another reader sends in a posting. And then another. And another. Discussions go on and on in this manner for days, creating a collection of articles on the same topic. When Usenet articles all refer to the same topic, they are organized into what is known as a "thread." To understand the ongoing discussion, it is essential to read a thread of articles in the order that they were posted.

Articles are all categorized according to so-called hierarchies of topics. The name of every newsgroup can be parsed according to the hierarchies, that is, from top-level categories to bottom-level categories. For example, the left-most part of a name indicates the top-most category or the most general category. Moving to the right, the topics become more specific. Some of the most common top-level categories are listed below.

Some Top-Level Newsgroup Categories

NAME	TOPIC
alt	Alternative
biz	Business
comp	Computer
k12	Grades Kindergarten through 12
rec	Recreation
sci	Science
soc	Social Issues

Many foreign language Usenet groups are indicated by a two-letter country code in the top-level category, that is, the left-most category. Consider the following names of two foreign news groups: **<fr.rec .cuisine>** and **<es.talk.politica>**. The first group is a French language group (fr.) about recreational cooking and dining. The second group is a Spanish language group (es.) devoted to the debate of political issues.

Deja News Site

Deja News tames the wild and woolly world of Usenet newsgroups with a user-friendly Web site available at **<http://www.dejanews.com/>**. Deja News essentially replaces the need for newsreader software by interfacing the Usenet service with the Web (see Figure 4.10). And

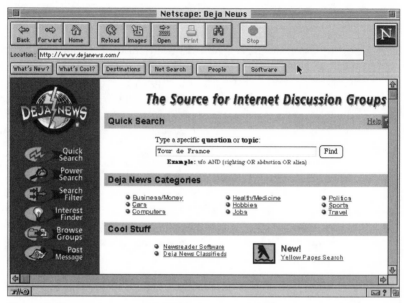

Figure 4.10

since you already know how to operate a browser, Deja News allows you to search, read, and participate in newsgroup discussions without needing any new software. Of course, after you have used Deja News to discover the Usenet and are no longer a novice, you may want to learn how to operate a newsreader. When that time comes, simply click on Netscape's handbook and read about Netscape News, Netscape Navigator's built-in newsreader. Until then, Deja News will give you access to any newsgroup that may interest you.

Deja News archives more than two years' worth of Usenet newsgroup postings—more than six times the content of the World Wide Web. In fact, Deja News searches the largest online text database in the world in only seconds. You can conduct a keyword search of the database for relevant articles. For example, a search conducted in August 1997 using the keyword phrase *"Tour de France"* resulted in 2,230 articles. As shown in Figure 4.11, pertinent information is given about every article including the article's subject, the newsgroup from which it came, and its author.

When you find an article that interests you, simply click on its link for the full text. For example, by clicking on the eleventh article in the list ("Tour de France féminin") you receive the text of Pierre Robert's article. In this case, Mr. Robert has posted a simple request in French asking about the existence of a Web site that covers the women's Tour de France (see Figure 4.12).

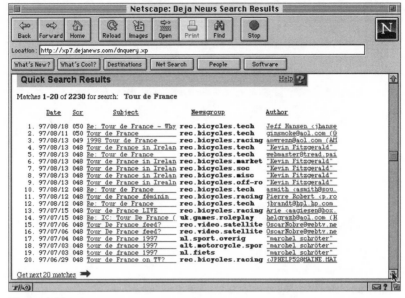

Figure 4.11

Figure 4.12

To view the thread to which this article belongs, that is, the collection of articles relating to the same topic, you have only to click on the link *View Thread*. Mr. Robert's message turns out to be an initial

query followed by a single reply. In other words, the article is the first
of a two-article thread (see Figure 4.13).

To read the reply, simply click on it. As shown in Figure 4.14,
Joe's answer in English is brief but informative: "The Tour Feminin

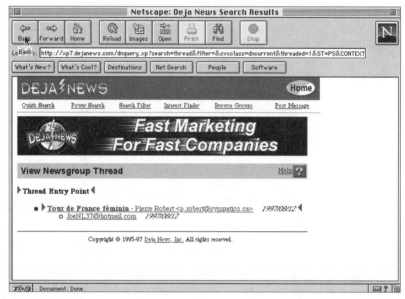

Figure 4.13

Figure 4.14

does not have its own site as far as I know, but you could try Cycle-Base for results etc." Note that the URL embedded in the posting is actually a hyperlink. If you click on it, you will go to CycleBase's homepage.

Several things should be clear from this short example. First, newsgroups are multilingual and multicultural. The question originally posted in French by a Canadian is answered in English by a native of the Netherlands. Second, newsgroups are wonderful places to ask for information about things of international interest. And third, Deja News makes reading newsgroup articles a very simple affair. If you wish to respond to an article, you need only to click on the link *Post Reply* . If you are posting an article for the first time, you will need to register with Deja News by leaving your email address.

The link *Browse Groups* allows you to examine the lists of newsgroups by subject category or hierarchy. For example, the *Regional* link gives you a list of foreign countries as well as all fifty states. Clicking on a country accesses a list of all the current newsgroups originating from that country. A quick browse through the countries indicates that there are hundreds of newsgroups in most of the major European languages: Spanish, French, German, Italian, Russian. And to help you get started, Deja News provides links just for novices. Be sure to check out the links *What Are Discussion Groups?* and *New Users!*

CHAT ROOMS

A final Internet resource for meeting and corresponding with speakers of other languages is the chat room. Chat rooms are sites on the Web where you can communicate with many other Web users at the same time in an extremely informal manner. They are generally characterized by a more or less simultaneous display of messages from every chat room participant. In other words, when you send a message to your fellow chat room denizens, it is posted for the entire chat room to see in a matter of seconds. The immediate posting of messages one after another simulates the turn taking of a live conversation and gives the unique feeling of chatting online with a roomful of other people.

Chat rooms are also generally characterized by the anonymity of the speakers who identify themselves by pseudonyms called "handles." While anonymity can contribute to a no-holds-barred exchange, it also limits the discussion in many ways. For example, because people are never identified, you rarely get to know them in any substantive way. Also, the discussion in chat rooms is free flowing; abrupt topic shifts are common as participants come and go. When you enter a chat room for the first time, you will be asked to register by giving some personal information such as your email

Figure 4.15

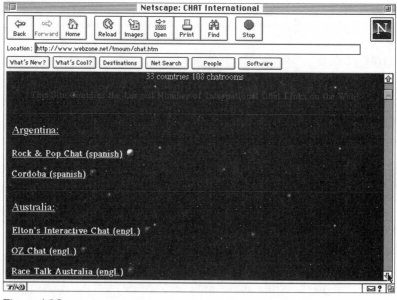

Figure 4.16

address, your full name, and a password. You may also need to download special software in order for the chat room messages to appear correctly on your screen.

Chat rooms are proliferating on the Web. A good place to begin is with Excite's People and Chat Channel at <**http://www.excite.com /channel/chat/**> (see Figure 4.15). Excite lists chat rooms by topics and by groups. Check out the link *Regional chat rooms* for international discussions.

Another place to experience multilingual chat is at Chat International. This Web site lists 108 different chat rooms in 33 different languages available at <**http://www.webzone.net/tmoum/chat.htm**> as shown in Figure 4.16.

You will have to visit several chat rooms until you find one that suits your style. And if you want to find more chat rooms, conduct a keyword search using the search engines discussed in Chapter 3.

Summary

In this chapter you have learned about five different ways to make online contact with speakers of other languages: personal email, pen pal Web sites, mailing lists, Usenet newsgroups, and chat rooms. Remember that whatever forum you ultimately try, all online communication will be greatly influenced by contextual factors such as the number of "speakers" participating in an interaction, the relationship of the "speakers" to each other, or the topic of discussion. In general, the different forums discussed in this chapter produce different kinds of interactions. You will undoubtedly have to experiment before you find a forum and a group of people with whom you feel comfortable. For example, you may find that the anonymity of a chat room allows you to broach topics that you would normally avoid or discuss in only the most circumspect manner. While chat rooms may, in some ways, be liberating, you may discover that what you really want is a more focused discussion where the ground rules are clearer and the participants' identities known. If that is the case, you may prefer joining a mailing list. Remember that there are thousands of different chat rooms, mailing lists, and newsgroups and that each one has its own personality. If you don't like one, try another.

From the point of view of language learning, you will have to see which forum suits your level of proficiency. If you are just beginning your study of Spanish for example, a Spanish language discussion of Mexican politics may be too challenging for you. Try another topic that is less technical or a group that accepts postings in both Spanish and English. Sometimes a bilingual context is more conducive to language learning since participants frequently ask each other for translations and clarifications. For example, you may find a Spanish-speaking pen pal who wants to practice her English. In this case, make a deal with her: She can write to you in English if you can write back in Spanish. This kind of bilingual exchange allows you both to practice using a foreign language while receiving corrective feedback so crucial to language learning.

On Your Own

A. Choose a search engine by selecting your browser's **Net Search** button and conduct a search for pen pal sites on the Web. Try combinations of the following keywords: *pen pal, pen friend, international correspondence, email pals, email networks, email discussion groups.* Can you find services with listings of pen pals who speak the language that you want to learn?

B. Select a pen pal site for closer inspection (either one of those discussed above or one from your own search of the Web).

1. Fill out an entry form and post it with the service. Carefully read all directions and rules for participation.

2. Find at least two pen pals with whom you would like to correspond. Send them an introductory email. Be sure to include a brief description of yourself and an explanation about why you wish to strike up a correspondence. And don't forget to mention how you got their email addresses.

C. Use several of the email search engines to look up the addresses of several of your friends. Verify the addresses of people who you know have an email account. Are their addresses available? Type in your name and see what information is listed about you in the various databases. Are you listed? Are your telephone number, street address, and email address correct?

D. Search Liszt at <http://www.liszt.com/> for a foreign language mailing list that interests you. You may be tempted to join several lists at once. Be careful. If you join several extremely active groups, you will find your mailbox flooded with messages. After you have found a list on a topic that interests you and that seems to suit your language needs, carefully read the directions for subscribing to that list. You will need to send a special email message to the *administrative address*. Remember to write the subscription message according to the exact specifications of the list. Subscription messages are usually a single line and include your name. How long does it take for you to get a response? Remember to save the first message from the list administrator, which includes important information including the list address for you to write to the other members. Save a copy of the list address for later use.

After a few weeks you will have a better sense of what the mailing list is all about, and you will know whether you wish to continue. How would you describe the group: active or inactive? friendly or argumentative? informative or dull? Is discussion mainly in one language? Is it a bilingual or multilingual list? If your mailing list is not very lively, you may want to remove your name by unsubscribing. Directions for unsubscribing are included in the initial email message you received from the list's administrator—the one that you carefully saved!

E. Peruse the lists of foreign language mailing lists and newsgroups at the Yamada Language Guides Web site at **<http://babel.uoregon.edu /yamada/guides.html>**. Are there languages with which you are unfamiliar? Compare some of the mailing lists according to the language. Do national and linguistic stereotypes hold true? Which nationality or language has the most discussion groups (mailing lists and newsgroups) devoted to wine? to cooking? to politics? to computers?

F. Visit Deja News at **<http://www.dejanews.com/>**. Click on *Browse Groups* located in the index to the left of the page. Next click on the link *Regional* for a listing of newsgroups by country. Browse the groups according to the language or country that interests you most. When you find an intriguing group, click on it and select an article thread. Start reading! What is the nature of the postings? Are they lengthy or short? Formal or informal?

After you have read around in several newsgroups you may start to recognize patterns of language use. Do you notice how the topic of discussion influences the way people interact? Are the political discussion groups more contentious than the groups devoted to leisure activities? Do people call each other names? Or do they remain civil while discussing controversial topics? Do people post articles in their native language or do they write in a foreign language? How can you tell? And can you parse the authors' email addresses?

After you have followed a newsgroup for several weeks, consider posting an article. Your posting may be a specific response to an earlier posting or it may be generally related to the discussion. See if your posting generates any response.

G. Visit the Web site Chat International at **<http://www.webzone.net /tmoum/chat.htm>**. Spend a few minutes in different chat rooms to get a feel for the kinds of topics discussed and the level of formality. You may want to begin by visiting the English language chat rooms before you try one in a foreign language. Chat rooms share many similarities with bars, pubs, or coffee houses; all are places where people go to meet and socialize. How do you strike up a conversation at those places? Do the same kinds of rules and rituals of face-to-face interaction apply to chat rooms or is it more like the telephone? Are you shy when you meet someone for the first time in a chat room or does the anonymity embolden you? What is the personality or atmosphere of the chat rooms? Can you guess the ages of the speakers by their use of language?

Chatting is a fairly informal speech act. Do you notice a lot of informal expressions and salutations, for example, "What's up?," "How's it going?," "Gotta run guys."? Might this be a good place to learn foreign language slang expressions? How many people are there in the room? How does the number of people affect the chatting? Do people split off into smaller groups of chatters? Do you feel yourself drawn to anyone in particular? Are there regulars, people who frequent the chat room on a regular basis?

A final word of advice: Remember that the atmosphere in a chat room depends almost entirely on the chemistry among the participants, in other words, whoever happens to drop in. Sometimes the chemistry is right and sometimes it isn't. You'll need patience and a little luck to find a chat room in which you feel comfortable; if at first you don't succeed, chat, chat again.

5 Sampling Online Foreign Language Resources

Foreign Language Learning Web Sites

Foreign Language Learning Tools
  Bilingual Dictionaries
  Directories
  Grammar and Vocabulary Lessons
  Pronunciation Guides
  Speech Synthesis
  Verb Conjugators
  Morphological Analysis
  Foreign Language Corpora
Foreign Language Schools
Foreign Language Career and Employment Services
Foreign Language Professional Organizations
Technology and Language Teaching Services

Foreign Language Web Sites of General Interest

Prado Museum
City.Net
German Information Center
Italia Online
Le Web du Tour de France
La Olla
Der Spiegel Online
LatinoWeb
Le ministère de la culture (France)
Numancia—La Ciudad Virtual
Les Champs Elysées Virtuels

Summary

As a foreign language learner, the best way for you to understand the enormous value of the Internet is to sample some of the online resources devoted to foreign languages and cultures. To that end, this chapter is essentially a "show and tell" of outstanding foreign language sites sorted into thematic categories and described in terms of their pedagogical value. Some Web sites featured here have been developed with the language learner in mind and have an explicit educational goal: for example, to teach the grammar or pronunciation of a language. Other sites are not for the foreign language learner per se, but nevertheless prove useful because they give the learner access to authentic samples of language as well as up-to-the-minute information about the target culture.

As you read this chapter, keep in mind that the selected sites do not constitute a representative sample of online resources, because the size of the Internet makes that task impossible. Instead, the sites have been chosen to give you a better idea of both the diversity and utility of online resources. They are but a fraction of what is currently available. Therefore, whatever the language of a featured site may be, chances are that there are other sites similar to it in a different language, even in less commonly taught languages like Arabic, Indonesian, or Chinese.

FOREIGN LANGUAGE LEARNING WEB SITES

In this section, you will learn about sites that have been created expressly for you, the foreign language learner. These sites have been developed to facilitate foreign language learning in some particular way. Some sites target primarily teachers or foreign language specialists, such as translators or interpreters, but contain much useful information for language learners.

Foreign Language Learning Tools

To learn a foreign language, students typically take advantage of various educational tools such as reference grammars, pronunciation guides, phrase books, and bilingual dictionaries. You will be pleased to know that these useful tools are now available online. But there are other online tools that you probably have never considered using, such as foreign language corpora, speech synthesis software, and electronic verb conjugators. All the tools featured in this chapter are free unless noted otherwise. They have been produced by foreign language educators for their students or by commercial enterprises as a free service to their customers.

Bilingual Dictionaries. The bilingual dictionary, a well-known language learning tool, can now be found in its electronic form on the Web. You already visited the most complete Web site for online dictionaries in Chapter 2: The Web of On-line Dictionaries Site.

<http://www.bucknell.edu/%7Erbeard/diction.html>

Another excellent site for online bilingual dictionaries is Travlang's Dictionary Site, which contains links to multilingual dictionaries of the major European languages. Although Travlang's dictionaries contain relatively few entries (anywhere from 5,000 to 10,000 words), they are all fast, easy to use, produce generally good results, and are perfect for the beginning language learner.

<http://dictionaries.travlang.com/>

And finally, to get a sense of the potential that technology holds for dictionaries, visit DicoVox's French/English bilingual dictionary with synthesized sounds for every entry. Not only does the dictionary give you an English translation for the French but it will pronounce the word for you too!

<http://latl.unige.ch/latl/dicovoxfe.html>

Directories.   You learned in Chapter 3 that one of the best places to find information on the Web is a directory, a site that organizes links by category. As the language lab of cassettes and headphones gives way to today's multimedia and computer center, many universities are developing their own foreign language learning Web directories. Here are a few of the very best:

Foreign Language Learning Center—Southern Methodist University

<http://fllc.smu.edu/>

Less Commonly Taught Languages Center—University of Minnesota

<http://carla.acad.umn.edu/lctl/lctl.html>

Computer Assisted Language Learning Lab—Ohio University

<http://www.tcom.ohiou.edu/OU_Language/OU_Language.html>

Foreign Language Resources on the Web—University of California at Berkeley

<http://www.itp.berkeley.edu/~thorne/HumanResources.html>

Romance Languages Resource Page—University of Chicago

<http://humanities.uchicago.edu/romance/>

Yamada Language Guides—University of Oregon

<http://babel.uoregon.edu/yamada/guides.html>

Grammar and Vocabulary Lessons.   Students who wish to brush up on their grammar will find a plethora of exercises and tutorials on the Web. Some of these online grammar materials are commercially produced, but most are components of university language courses. For example, the Spanish and French programs at the University of Texas at Austin offer complete interactive grammar and vocabulary exercises. Type in your answers and click for the corrections.

First-Year College French Grammar/Vocabulary Exercises

<http://www2.sp.utexas.edu/fr/student.qry>

First-Year College Spanish Grammar/Vocabulary Exercises

<http://www2.sp.utexas.edu/SP506/student.qry>

La página de la lengua española: an excellent list of Spanish language online lessons.

<http://www.dat.etsit.upm.es/~mmonjas/gram.html>

TennesseeBob's Famous French Links: a spectacular directory of over 130 online French language courses for all levels.

<http://globegate.utm.edu/french/globegate_mirror
/frlesson.html>

German for Beginners: a complete online German language course.

<http://castle.uvic.ca/german/149/>

A Web of Online Grammars: the Web's most complete and diverse list of foreign language grammars (literally from Akkadian to Wolof). You will find a wide variety of grammars at this site: pedagogical grammars, reference grammars, formal grammars for linguists.

<http://www.bucknell.edu/%7Erbeard/grammars.html>

Pronunciation Guides.   Pronunciation lessons are an essential component of the foreign language curriculum. Most sites include brief descriptions of the sounds of a language, accompanied by clickable sound files. Sound files come in several different varieties. They can usually be played directly using your browser and a plug-in. Verify that you have the correct plug-in to play the file. If you do not, you may need to download the appropriate sound plug-in. You also may want to download the foreign language files onto your hard disk for practice later.

Travlang's Foreign Languages for Travelers is a commercial site where you will find phrasebooks with recordings in over fifty languages. Just click on the flag icon of the language you want to hear pronounced.

<http://www.travlang.com/languages/>

Español para Viajeros is one of the guides you will find at the above Web site. The Spanish pronunciation guide has hundreds of high quality recordings in the following categories: Palabras Básicas (Basic Words), Números (Numbers), Compras (Shopping), Comidas (Dining), Viajar (Travel), Direcciones (Directions), Lugares (Place Names), Fechas y Horas (Dates and Times). Be careful to type in the long URL exactly as it appears.

<http://www.travlang.com/languages/cgi-bin/langchoice
.cgi?page=main&lang1=english&flags.x=312&flags.y=33>

French Phonetics, Listening, Pronunciation and Conversation Page contains a complete listing of courses about the French sound system. Another TennesseeBob special.

<http://globegate.utm.edu/french/globegate_mirror/oral.html>

German Pronunciation is a complete online course for beginning German students originating from a server at the College of William and Mary.

<http://www.wm.edu/CAS/modlang/gasmit/pronunciation
/pronunce.html>

Kiswahili Pronunciation Course is part of an online Swahili course developed for students at Yale University.

<http://www.cis.yale.edu:80/swahili/sound/pronunce.htm>

Speech Synthesis.   Speech synthesis is an emerging technology with obvious applications to language learning. Imagine being able to type a foreign word or phrase and then hear the computer read it back to you. If such a possibility intrigues you, visit these sites, which contain links to over a hundred human communication research centers with fascinating online resources for both speech synthesis and voice recognition.

Speech on the Web includes links to speech synthesis labs as well as corpora of spoken French, English, and Dutch.

<http://www.tue.nl/ipo/hearing/webspeak.htm#On-line>

The Museum of Speech Synthesis in French (Musée sonore de la synthèse de la Parole en français) Located in Grenoble, France, it includes some of the best online speech synthesis software currently available. Most software is available only in demo form, although some software is downloadable for free. Read the directions carefully. You will probably need to download browser plug-ins to make these software programs run correctly on your computer.

<http://ophale.icp.grenet.fr/exFr.html>

AT&T Speech Lab allows you to listen to speech synthesized in various languages and in various voices. Whose voice do you prefer? A man's? A woman's? A small child's?

<http://www.research.att.com/cgi-usr/mjm/voices.cgi>

Verb Conjugators.   Do irregular verb forms drive you crazy? Have you ever been at a loss for the correct conjugation of the imperfect subjunctive? If so, you will find a verb conjugator to be just what you need. At these two sites, you can conjugate a verb by entering the infinitive form of the verb in the box. (If you don't know the infinitive form of the verb, use one of the bilingual dictionaries discussed above.) The conjugator will supply you with all forms of the verb.

French Verb Conjugator

<http://tuna.uchicago.edu/forms_unrest/inflect.query.html>

Spanish Verb Conjugator

<http://csgwww.uwaterloo.ca/~dmg/lando/verbos
/con-jugador.html>

Morphological Analysis.   Not only can computers conjugate verbs, they can also parse sentences. A morphological analyzer gives you a context-free grammatical analysis for every word or string of words you enter. Morphological analyzers are currently being developed by linguists for many different languages. Because the technology is still new and the interfaces not very user friendly, present versions of morphological analyzers may hold more appeal for professional linguists and foreign language specialists than for learners.

The INFL Morphological Analyzer will automatically give you grammatical information about every word in a French sentence. Unfortunately, the grammatical information is a bit too cryptic and opaque for most beginning French students. However, it may be of use to advanced students. Even if you find this tool inaccessible in its present version, this site is worth a visit to see how technology is changing the field of language studies.

<http://humanities.uchicago.edu/forms_unrest/analyze.query.html>

Foreign Language Corpora.   Corpora (the plural of corpus) are large collections of linguistic data, either written texts or transcriptions of recorded speech, which can be used in many ways by language learners and teachers. Most learners find example sentences extremely useful for understanding grammar and language use. In fact, learners often admit that they prefer example sentences to a textbook's technical explanations of the grammar. Well, with a computerized corpus, you can access hundreds of example sentences illustrating the use of a particular grammatical construction or vocabulary item.

The Corpus Linguistics Site originating from Rice University contains links to corpora in many different languages, including samples of written and spoken language. Many of the corpora accessible from this site are searchable by keyword. Simply type in a foreign word and you will receive contextualized examples of that word as it appears in the corpus. In addition to collections of authentic foreign language samples of speech and writing, you will find links to the O. J. Simpson trial courtroom transcripts and other strange and interesting corpora.

<http://www.ruf.rice.edu/~barlow/corpus.html>

The American and French Research on the Treasury of the French Language Project, more commonly referred to by its acronym ARTFL, is a joint corpus project undertaken by the Centre Nationale de la Recherche Scientifique (France) and the University of Chicago. At present the ARTFL corpus includes nearly 2,000 texts, ranging from classic works of French literature to various kinds of nonfiction prose and technical writing. The corpus is one of the largest of its kind in the world, totaling some 150 million words and representing a broad range of written French stretching from the seventeenth to the twentieth centuries. According to the developers of the Web site, the ARTFL corpus permits both the rapid exploration of a single text or the comparison of many different texts. Besides the corpus, the ARTFL Web site contains many other resources and bibliographic information for the serious student of the French language.

<http://humanities.uchicago.edu/ARTFL/ARTFL.html#general>

Foreign Language Schools

Language schools are an obvious resource for anyone wishing to learn a foreign language. Today, many schools maintain Web sites that include valuable materials for and about language learning.

Goethe Institute promotes the study of the German language and culture abroad. At this site, you will find all the information you need about the Institute's courses at over sixty campuses: schedules, prices, locations, and registration. Even if you don't want to sign up for a course, you can download German language materials. A useful site for German students and teachers.

<http://www.goethe.de/>

French Schools Around the World contains a list of French language schools both public and private.

<http://www.sfu.ca/cprf/ecoles.html>

Sí Spain's University Page lists Spanish universities that offer Spanish language courses for foreigners.

<http://www.DocuWeb.ca/SiSpain/english/educatio
/connecti.html>

Foreign Language Career and Employment Services

Have you ever wondered what kind of career opportunities there are in the field of foreign languages? If you are a beginning foreign language student you may think that it is a bit premature to start planning a foreign language career. Nevertheless, perusing job openings can give you insights about the field of foreign languages that may prove valuable and motivating.

Employment Resources for Language Teachers is a site for foreign language teachers (including English as a Second or Foreign Language) who are looking for work in the United States and around the world. In addition to a list of useful job links, there is a selection of prestructured Web searches to help you find the teaching job of your dreams. Tell your teacher about it.

<**http://www.tcom.ohiou.edu/OU_Language/teacher/job.html**>

Foreign Language Professional Organizations

If you are a student of German (or Spanish, or French, or some other language), you probably haven't considered visiting the Web site of a professional organization such as the American Association of Teachers of German. But you should. You will find that such sites offer an excellent array of links to all kinds of foreign language materials and services that are as useful to you as to your teachers.

American Council on the Teaching of Foreign Languages (ACTFL)

<**http://www.actfl.org/**>

American Association of Teachers of German (AATG)

<**http://www.aatg.org/**>

American Association of Teachers of French (AATF)

<**http://aatf.utsa.edu/**>

American Association of Teachers of Spanish and Portuguese (AATSP)

<**http://www.aatsp.org/home.html**>

English Language Teaching Professional Organizations

<**http://www.tcom.ohiou.edu/OU_Language/teacher /groupEnglish.html**>

Technology and Language Teaching Services

Educational technology is having a tremendous impact on foreign language learning. While publishing companies and educational institutions are producing more and more sophisticated foreign language CD-ROMs and Web tutorials to supplement and extend the curriculum, students may not always know how to use these technologies most effectively. The Web is an excellent place to learn more about what technologies are currently available and how various technologies can be used to improve your linguistic proficiency.

Technology and Language Teaching Page (Ohio University) includes educational technology links for the following: mailing groups, news-groups, foreign language learning software sites, professional organizations, journals, and university foreign language technology labs.

<http://www.tcom.ohiou.edu/OU_Language/teacher
/technology.html>

FOREIGN LANGUAGE WEB SITES OF GENERAL INTEREST

If you are like many language students, you may question the value of surfing Web sites that have been designed for native foreign language speakers. Won't the language be too difficult for you to understand? Won't there be too many cultural allusions that will escape you? Shouldn't you stick to the security of your textbook? The answer to all these questions is, in a word, no! Web sites that have been developed by and for native speakers can be of tremendous value to foreign language learners—even beginners. You should view them as documents that deserve to be studied for their fascinating cultural and linguistic information. On the other hand, foreign language documents do present special difficulties for learners and should be chosen with a few special criteria in mind.

All the sites featured here have been selected because they follow some basic principles of good design. First, they all make liberal use of photos and graphics. A picture can truly be worth a thousand words, especially when those words are in a foreign language. A good Web site for foreign language learning should have a certain amount of redundancy between the photos and the text, that is, photos and text should contextualize each other. Second, many of the Web sites shown here are bilingual, available in a foreign language version and an English version (some sites are multilingual). Just click on the appropriate link or icon, for example, the American or British flag. Third, to be accessible to foreign language learners, Web sites must have an interface that is relatively simple, clean, and easy to use. You should not have to spend a lot of time trying to figure out how to navigate a site or what you are supposed to do once you are there. And finally, all the sites sampled in this chapter are fun and creative, engaging your imagination as well as your intellect.

Prado Museum

<http://museoprado.mcu.es/>

Figure 5.1

The Prado in Madrid is home to some of the most famous art treasures in the world. Fortunately, its magnificent collections are now available online. Begin your visit to this wonderful Web site by taking a guided tour (in Spanish or in English) of the museum's fifty most important works. Each month the Web site features the work of a single artist, which is analyzed in depth by the Prado's curators. There are also links to online activities and courses to increase your knowledge of the art collections as well as the history of this great museum.

City.Net

<http://www.city.net/>

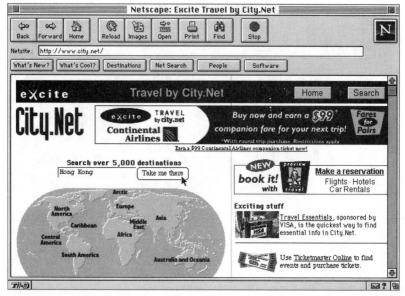

Figure 5.2

City.Net is a Web site that every foreign language student should know about. This amazing Web site allows you to take a virtual tour of over 5,000 cities. Simply type in the name of the city or country you wish to visit and off you go. But City.Net is much more than sightseeing tours of famous monuments. You will also find links to information in English and in the city's native language(s) about hotels, restaurants, shopping, transportation, maps, entertainment, and media sources. In short, City.Net provides the best and most up-to-date travel information on the Web.

German Information Center

<http://www.germany-info.org/>

Figure 5.3

Under the auspices of the German Foreign Ministry and the Federal Press and Information Office, the German Information Center's main goal is to provide media services and materials about Germany. The Center's Web site disseminates information on all aspects of German society: political, economic, and cultural. Two German language weekly newsletters and several nonperiodical publications are available online. German language students will especially appreciate the links *Germany in the US* and the *Student Corner*, which provide information about student exchanges and study abroad programs.

Italia Online

<http://www.iol.it/>

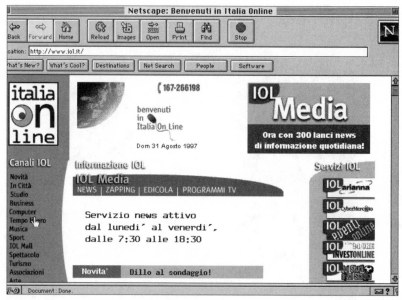

Figure 5.4

Web surfing Italian style! This visually stunning Web site brings you modern Italy—politics, television, cinema, fashion, business, newspapers, music, cooking, sports—like nothing else. If it is happening in Italy, it's on *Italia Online*. Students will love the lively chat rooms and newsgroups. This site is as much fun as it is educational.

Le Web du Tour de France

<http://www.letour.com/home.html>

Figure 5.5

The thrill of victory and the agony of defeat. You don't need to be a cycling enthusiast or a French speaker to enjoy this spectacular sports site. Be sure to check out the animated maps of this most famous of cycling races. Click anywhere on the race's route and you will be presented with a detailed representation of the altitude and road conditions the cyclists must endure at that point in the race. There is also a bank of video highlights from French television arranged in chronological order.

La Olla

<http://www.telebase.es/laolla/menu.htm>

Figure 5.6

Do you want to try your hand at preparing paella? Would you like some new ideas for tapas? And what are the tricks for making the perfect flan? *Olla* is an electronic cookbook featuring hundreds of classic Spanish recipes. *Olla* is as much a feast for the eyes as it is for the stomach; every dish is beautifully illustrated and described in detail. There are also links to other Spanish cooking sites.

Der Spiegel Online

<http://www.spiegel.de/>

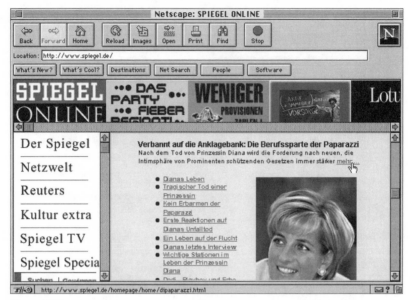

Figure 5.7

German students can now enjoy Germany's most popular news magazine on the Web. An excellent source of news about Germany, *Der Spiegel* also provides the Reuters International News service in German. *Der Spiegel Online* will also permit searches of all its back issues.

LatinoWeb

<http://www.catalog.com/favision/latnoweb>

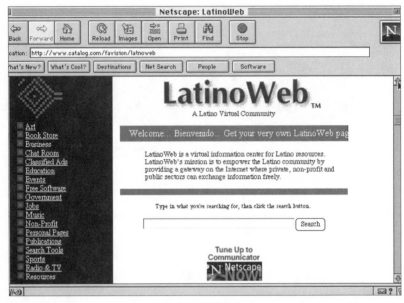

Figure 5.8

Foreign language learners can immerse themselves in a language and culture by visiting so-called virtual communities, places on the Internet where members of a language community exchange information freely. These sites typically combine easy access to current information important to members of a community as well as various forums for communication among members: chat rooms, bulletin board services, and listservs. An excellent example of a virtual community is LatinoWeb, whose stated mission is to "empower the Latino community by providing a gateway on the Internet where private, non-profit and public sectors can exchange information freely." If you don't want to waste time surfing the Web for related language and culture sites about the Latino community, visit LatinoWeb, where you'll find everything in one convenient place.

Le ministère de la culture (France)

<http://www.culture.fr/>

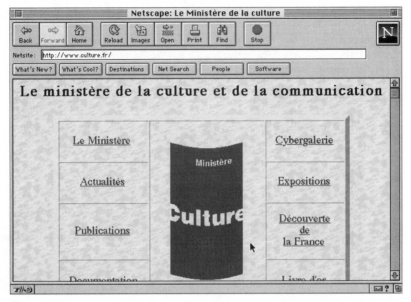

Figure 5.9

Students of French culture should not miss this Web site, which includes links to France's most famous art museums and galleries. French students will not only appreciate the excellent art exhibits, but because this is an official governmental office, they will gain insight here into the role of art in modern French society, and in particular, the political role of the Ministry of Culture.

Numancia—La Ciudad Virtual

<http://www.laeff.esa.es/~crb/Numancia.html>

Figure 5.10

Numancia is a virtual Spanish city complete with barrios and a "Plaza Mayor." Visiting Numancia is akin to playing a Spanish computer game. As you wander the streets of this imaginary city, you never know who you will run into or what you will find. You can even communicate with the inhabitants of Numancia—in Spanish, of course.

Les Champs Elysées Virtuels

<http://www.iway.fr/champs-elysees/>

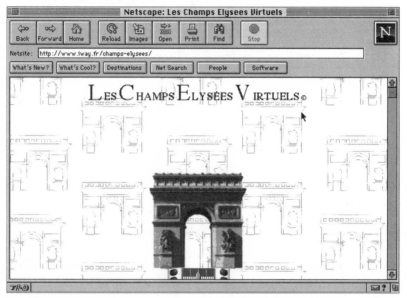

Figure 5.11

At this clever site, French students can get a feel for Paris by taking a virtual "scroll" from one end of the avenue to the other. As you walk along the sidewalk be sure to click on the famous stores and restaurants for a virtual tour: Renault, Club Med, Crédit Lyonnais, Peugeot, Espace mode, le Drugstore.

Summary

The purpose of this chapter was to give you an overview of online foreign language learning resources. Remember that the sites featured above are only a tiny fraction of those currently available. Moreover, since the Web is growing at such an astounding pace, it is certain that even more foreign language resources will be available in the future. By reading about the sites featured in this chapter, you can now understand why so many people—both learners and teachers—are convinced that cyberspace is an excellent place to learn a foreign language. After all, the Web allows you to communicate with the world in a way that has never before been possible. And that's not hype, that's fact.

Glossary

The language of the Internet includes technical terms, jargon, and even slang, and some of it may be quite new to you. If you have little or no experience using the Internet for research, take some time to read through the glossary. As you come across terms or concepts that need clarification, you'll find help here. You'll also encounter many of these terms again and again as you use the Internet—and as you use *Untangling the Web*.

< > (angle brackets)   Angle brackets around text indicate that all the characters within the brackets must be treated as a single unit, with no spaces between parts, as in <http://www.infolink.org/glossary.htm>. By using angle brackets to frame handwritten or printed electronic information (e.g., email addresses and Web site locations), you prevent misinterpretation. Omit the angle brackets when you type URLs or email addresses into your browser's or email program's dialog box.

@ (the "at" sign)   A fixture in every email address, @ separates the username from the domain name, indicating that you are "at" a particular electronic address. For example, <jhsmith@acs.eku.edu> indicates that someone, possibly Jane Smith, gets email at Academic Computing Services, which is at Eastern Kentucky University, an educational institution. See also *email* and *email address*.

. (the dot)   The period symbol, called "the dot" in online lingo, is used to separate parts of email addresses, URLs, and newsgroup names, as in <jhsmith@acs.eku.edu>, <http://www.yahoo.com>, and <alt.sci.ecology>.

/ (the forward slash)   Used to separate parts of URLs, as in <ftp://ftp.tidbits.com/pub>; not to be confused with the backward slash \ used in DOS directory paths.

account name   See *username*.

Archie   An Internet search tool for finding and retrieving computer files from archives.

Thanks to Andrew Harnack and Eugene Kleppinger, who prepared this glossary for their Internet guide *Online! A Reference Guide to Using Internet Sources*, also published by St. Martin's Press (1997). Used with permission. Visit their Web site: <www.smpcollege.com/online-4styles~help>.

archive   A collection of computer files stored on a server. FTP sites are typical examples of archives.

article   Internet lingo for a message posted online.

ASCII   An acronym for American Standard Code for Information Interchange, ASCII is the most basic format for transferring files between different programs. It is sometimes referred to in word-processing programs as "unformatted text."

asynchronous communication   Electronic communication involving messages that are posted and received at different times. Email is an example of such delayed communication.

BBS (bulletin board service)   A service maintained by a computer that serves as an information hub for many computers. People with common interests subscribe to a BBS in order to post and receive messages.

bookmark   An entry in a bookmark list.

bookmark list   A browser's pulldown menu or popup window containing links to Web sites you want to visit frequently; sometimes called a *hotlist*.

browser   A World Wide Web program for navigating the Internet. Most browsers display graphics and formatted pages and let you click on hyperlinks to "jump" from one Web page to another. Widely used *graphic browsers* include HotJava, Microsoft Explorer, NCSA Mosaic, and Netscape Navigator. A popular *text-only browser* is Lynx.

bulletin board service   See *BBS*.

client   A requester of information. As you surf the Internet, you, your computer, or your browser may be considered an Internet client.

cyber-   A prefix describing something that has been created electronically and is available online (e.g., a *cyberworld*, a *cybercity*, a *cyberstore*). *Cyber* can also stand alone as an adjective, especially to avoid clunky compounds: *cyber rights, cyber cowboy, cyber pipe dreams*.

cyberography   A list of references to Internet sites.

cyberspace   The Internet; more loosely, the online world.

dialog box   A window on your computer screen that prompts you to type something, make choices, or confirm a command before the program can continue.

digital   Electronic; "wired."

direct access   A computer connection that lets you use Internet software (e.g., a graphic browser) on your personal computer.

directory   A list or collection of related computer files, sometimes called a *folder*. A directory may contain other directories, which are then called *subdirectories*.

directory path   The sequence of directories and subdirectories you need to open to find a particular computer file. For example, the directory path <pub\data\history> shows that the *history* file is in the *data* subdirectory, which in turn is in the *pub* directory.

domain   See *domain name*.

domain name   The string of letters and symbols associated with a Web site or email service provider, as in <www.enigmacom.com>. A domain name has at least two *elements* (parts), separated by periods. The first element or elements uniquely identify an organization's server, while the final element, called the *domain*, identifies the type of organization operating the server. Common suffixes include *.com* (commercial), *.edu* (educational), *.gov* (government), *.mil* (military), *.net* (network management), and *.org* (noncommercial/nonprofit). Domains outside the United States often identify the country in which a server is located (e.g., *.au* for Australia, *.ch* for Switzerland).

download   To transfer information electronically from one computer to another, as when you move a program from an archive to your computer.

email (electronic mail)   Any of various programs that send and receive messages over a network.

email address   The address you use to send and receive email. Your email address contains your username, the @ symbol, and the domain name, as in <jhsmith@acs.eku.edu>.

emoticons   Small graphic renderings, composed of ASCII characters, that writers substitute for facial expressions and body language. Emoticons are useful in an online world where curt or hastily written messages can easily offend, and where you may want to indicate humor, surprise, or some other emotion to readers who cannot see you.

FAQ (frequently asked questions)   Pronounced "fack"; a file containing answers to common questions that new users of a program or service might ask. If you are new to a newsgroup or listserv, look up the group's FAQ file and read the answers to questions others have already asked.

FTP (file transfer protocol)   The set of commands used to transfer files between computers on the Internet.

GIF (graphics interchange format)   Pronounced "jiff" or "giff"; one of two common formats (the other is *JPEG)* for image files associated with Web documents. The acronym appears at the end of the filename, as in <marsface.gif>.

gopher   A program for accessing Internet information through hierarchical menus, gopher will "go for" the information you select and will display it on your screen. When you use gopher through direct access, with a graphic browser, you choose menu items by clicking your computer's mouse. When you use gopher through indirect access, the menu lists choices by line number, and you select what you want using keyboard commands. Gopher's text-oriented file format makes it especially useful for searching large collections of texts such as electronic books, library catalogs, historical documents, and specialized databases. On the World Wide Web, gopher addresses begin with *gopher://* instead of *http://* .

history list   A list (usually a pulldown menu) of the Web pages you most recently visited. History lists let you return quickly to a site or see an overview of your latest surfing session.

hit   In Internet lingo, hit can mean (1) an item in the list of search results a browser gives you ("AltaVista's search for *scorpions* turned up sixty-nine hits"), or (2) accessing of a Web page by an Internet surfer ("The UT-Austin French Web page received three hundred hits this week").

homepage   Usually the first page you see when you access a particular Web site, a homepage has hypertext links to other pages on the same server or to other Web servers. Both organizations and individuals can have their own homepages.

hotlink   See *hyperlink.*

hotlist   See *bookmark list.*

HTML (hypertext markup language)   A computer code that allows you to create pages on the World Wide Web. HTML "tags" electronic text to indicate how it should be displayed onscreen by browsers. It provides a common language for browsers using different computer systems (Mac, PC, Unix, etc.).

HTTP (hypertext transfer protocol) The communication rules used by browsers and servers to move HTML documents across the Web.

hyperlink A connection between two places on the Web. Hyperlinks are represented onscreen by highlighted icons or text. Selecting a hyperlink makes your browser "jump" from one place to another. Hyperlinks are sometimes called *hotlinks*.

HyperNews A format that lets Web pages offer articles to read and gives readers special tools for responding online to articles and responses already posted by others. In HyperNews, all contributions are automatically added to the Web page, whose topically arranged menu gives convenient access to *threads* (ongoing discussions on specific topics).

hypertext A document coded in HTML; a collection of such documents.

hypertext link A connection between two documents or sections of a document on the Web; a type of *hyperlink*.

hypertext markup language See *HTML*.

hypertext transfer protocol See *HTTP*.

indirect access A computer connection that lets you run Internet programs stored on another computer system; also called *shell access*.

Internet A vast network of computers offering many types of services, including email and access to the World Wide Web. As a "network of networks," the Internet links computers around the world.

Internet service provider (ISP) A person or company providing access to the Internet.

IRC (Internet relay chat) The online equivalent of CB radio and telephone conferencing, IRC lets you communicate synchronously (in "real time") with other people. See also *synchronous communication*.

ISP See *Internet service provider.*

JPEG (Joint Photographic Experts Group) Pronounced "jay-peg"; one of two common formats (the other is GIF) for image files associated with Web documents. In filenames the acronym appears as *jpeg* or *jpg,* as in <pluto.jpg>.

keyword   The term you type into a search tool's dialog box; what you want to search for.

linkage data   Information about the hypertext context in which a document is located (i.e., the document's links to other documents).

listserv   An ongoing email discussion about a technical or nontechnical issue. Participants subscribe via a central service, and listservs may have a moderator who manages information flow and content.

modem   Equipment that connects a computer to a data transmission line (usually a telephone line), enabling the computer to communicate with other computers and the Internet.

MOO (multi-user domain, object-oriented)   An electronic "space" in which many people can interact simultaneously. Accessible through telnet, MOOs enable classes, seminars, and friends to meet at a given time, usually to discuss a given topic.

MUD (multi-user domain)   As electronic "spaces" for simultaneous communication, MUDs provide opportunities for role-playing in which each participant usually controls one character who has a complete life history and persona and can express a variety of physical and emotional responses.

netiquette   A combination of the words *Net* and *etiquette, netiquette* refers to appropriate behavior on a network, and more generally the Internet.

newbie   A new Internet user.

newsgroup   A group of people and their collection of postings on the Usenet network. Newsgroups are open forums in which anyone may participate. Each newsgroup has a topic, which can be as broad as the focus of <alt.activism> or as narrow as the computer applications discusssed in <comp.sys.mac.apps>. See also *Usenet.*

online   On a network; on the Internet.

password   A personal code you use to access your computer account and keep it private.

post   To send a message to someone online. An online message is a *posting.*

protocol   A set of commands—the "language"—that computers use to exchange information. Often-used protocols include FTP, gopher, HTTP, mailto, and telnet.

real-time communication   See *synchronous communication.*

search engine   Any of various programs that work with your browser to find information on the Web. After you type a keyword or keywords into your browser's dialog box, a search engine looks for Web pages containing your keyword(s) and produces a menu of available documents (hits). Also called *search tool.*

server   A computer that handles requests from client computers for data, email, file transfer, and other network services.

shell access   See *indirect access.*

snail mail   The U.S. Postal Service or another agency that delivers messages by courier.

subject directory   A hypertext list of available Web sites categorized by subject; what you get when you use search engines such as Yahoo! or The Internet Services List.

surf   To navigate the Internet. A *surfer* is an avid Internet user.

synchronous communication   Electronic communication in which people converse simultaneously with one another; also called *real-time communication.* MOOs, MUDs, and IRCs are examples of synchronous communication.

TCP/IP   An abbreviation for *transmission control protocol/Internet protocol,* TCP/IP controls software applications on the Internet.

telnet   A program that lets you log onto another computer from your own computer using a username and a password.

text index   A hypertext list of Web sites containing the keyword(s) you specify; what you get when you use search engines such as Lycos or AltaVista.

thread   A series of postings about a particular topic. For example, you might decide to follow a *fire ants* thread in the newsgroup <alt.sci.ecology>.

URL (uniform resource locator)   Pronounced "u-r-l." A string of characters that uniquely identifies each page of information on the World Wide Web; a Web address.

Usenet   A network providing access to electronic discussion groups (newsgroups). You can join any of thousands of Usenet newsgroups by using a newsreader program.

Usenet newsgroup   See *newsgroup.*

username   The information that, combined with your password, lets you access your computer account; also called *account name,* *userid*. Your Internet email address probably begins with your username.

Veronica   An acronym for Very Easy Rodent-Oriented Net-Wide Index to Computerized Archives. Veronica is a program that searches for files over all available gopher servers on the Internet.

virtual   Online; occurring or existing in cyberspace.

WAIS (Wide Area Information Server)   A program that searches a variety of Internet databases by looking for specific keywords in documents rather than simply looking at document titles.

Web   See *World Wide Web*.

Web browser   See *browser*.

Web site   Any location on the World Wide Web.

wired   Electronic; online.

World Wide Web (WWW)   A global Internet service connecting hypertext data and resources. Using a browser, you can move quickly from one Web site to another in search of information, graphics, and data.

To find out more about Internet terms, consult the following Web resources:

Wired Style

> \<http://www.hotwired.com/hardwired/wiredstyle\>

Internet Glossary

> \<http://www.macintoshos.com/internet.connectivity/internet.glossary.html\>

Internet Glossary of Terms

> \<http://www.sparknet.net/spark_html/glossary.html\>

Web Info Internet Glossary

> \<http://www.infolink.org/glossary.htm\>

Glossary of Web-Related Terms for French, German, and Spanish

As you glance through the Web-related terminology in French, German, and Spanish, you will quickly see that English is the lingua franca of the computer world. For better or worse, English dominates the way most people throughout the globe talk about the Web.

These brief glossaries provide you with a starting point for talking about the Internet in French, German, and Spanish. They are not meant to be a definitive or exclusive list. Any attempt to produce a definitive list of foreign language terminology about the Net would be foolhardy. Languages change, borrow, and invent new words all the time, and nowhere does this happen more quickly and dramatically than in terminology referring to technology.

Different people have different relationships to their own language and to the languages of other cultures. This often produces strong feelings about the acceptability of incorporating nonnative words and expressions into one's own language, and native speakers of a language will often argue about which of the terms is "better, more authentic, or absolutely correct." The terminology of the Web varies greatly and you, like the native speakers of other languages, will have to find common terms to express the meaning you intend. So here you have our guide. It will help get you started on the information superhighway, which is dotted with traffic signs in many different languages.

French

ENGLISH	FRENCH
< > (angle brackets)	les crochets
@	arobase
. (dot)	puce
account	le compte
alias	le surnom, l'alias
anonymous FTP	FTP anonyme
Archie	Archie
archive	l'archive
article	l'article
ASCII	ASCII
attachment	annexe
backup	sauvegarde
bandwidth	la bande passante

BBS	le Babel (BABillard électronique), BAB, BBS
bookmark	le signet, l'onglet, la marque-page
bookmark list	la liste de signets
browser	le navigateur, le butineur, le feuilleteur; fureteur (Québec)
bug	le bogue, le pépin
click	cliquer (v)
client	le client
cyberspace	le Cyberespace, le Cybermonde
digital	digital
direct access	l'accès direct
directory	répertoire
domain name	le nom de domaine
download	téléchargement; importer, télécharger (v)
drag	glisser (v)
electronic mail	le courrier électronique
email	l'E-mail, CE
email address	l'adresse courrier électronique
emoticon	la mimique; la binette (Québec)
FAQ	FAQ (Foire Aux Questions)
flame	flamber (v)
folder	le dossier
forward	faire suivre (v)
freeware	le gratuicel, le graticiel
FTP	le FTP (Protocole de transfert de fichiers)
GIF	le GIF
gopher	le Gopher, la fouine
hacker	le finaud, le bidouilleur
hit	l'accès
homepage	la page d'accueil, la page de base
host	(le serveur) hôte
hostname	le nom d'hôte
hotlist	la liste de signets, le mémo de signets
HTML	HTML (langage hypertexte à balises)
HTTP	HTTP
hyperlink	l'hyperlien

hypertext	l'hypertexte
hypertext link	le lien hypertexte
Internet	l'Internet
IP address	l'adresse IP
IRC	l'IRC (causerie en temps réel)
keyword	le not clé
listserv	le serveur de listes
login	le nom de conexion, le nom d'utilisateur, l'entrée dans le système
logoff	la fin de session
mailbox	la boîte aux lettres, BAL, Blé (boîte aux lettres électronique)
mailing list	la liste de diffusion, le forum électronique
mirror site	le site miroir
modem	le modem
netiquette	la nétiquette, l'etiquette Usenet
newsgroup	le newsgroup, le News, le Forum, le groupe de discussion, le groupe de nouvelles
newsreader	le lecteur de nouvelles
online	en ligne
password	le mot de passe, le password
postmaster	le maître de poste, le postier, le chef de poste
plug-in	la module d'extension, l'accesoire
prompt	l'invite
protocol	le protocole
real-time communication (chat)	la causerie en temps réel
search engine	la moteur de recherche
search tool	l'outil de recherche
server	le serveur
shareware	le partagiciel
shell	l'interpréteur de commandes
snail mail	le courrier postal, le courrier escargot
software	le logiciel
surf	surfer (v)
synchronous communication	la communication synchrone

TCP/IP	TCP/IP
telnet	le telnet
thread	l'enfilade, la série
toolbar	la barre d'outils
upload	le dépôt, exporter (v)
URL	l'adresse URL (Locateur Uniforme de Ressource)
Usenet	le lecteur Usenet, lecteur nouvelles
username	le nom d'utilisateur
Web	le Web, W3
Web browser	
Webmaster	le Webmaîstre
WWW	le Web, W3, hypertoile

German

ENGLISH	GERMAN
< > (angle brackets)	die Eckigen Klammern
@	der Klammeraffe
. (dot)	der Punkt
/ (forward slash)	der Schrägstrich
alias	der Alias
anonymous FTP	das anonyme FTP
Archie	Archie
archive	das Archiv
article	der Artikel
ASCII	ASCII
asynchronous communication	die asynchrone Verbindung, die asynchrone Kommunikation
BBS	BBS
bandwidth	die Bandbreite
bookmark	das Bookmark, das Lesezeichen
browser	der Browser
client	der Client
cyberspace	Cyberspace
dialog box	Dialogbox
digital	digital

direct access	Direktzugriff
directory	das Verzeichnis
domain name	der Domain-Name, die Domäne
download	das Herunterladen, download
electronic mail	die Elektronische Post
email	die eMail, E-Mail
email address	eMail-Adresse
emoticon	das Emoticon
FAQ	FAQ
flame	der Flame
freeware	die Freeware
FTP	das FTP
GIF	GIF
gopher	der Gopher
hacker	der Hacker
history list	die Historie
hit	der Treffer
homepage	die Home Page
host	der Host, der Gastgeber
HTML	die HTML
HTTP	das HTTP
hyperlink	der Hyperlink, der Querverweis
hypertext	der Hypertext
hypertext link	der Hypertextlink, der Hypertext-Verweis
icon	Icon, Sinnbild
indirect access	der indirekter Zugriff
Internet	das Internet
IP address	die IP-Adresse
IRC	IRC
ISP	ISP
JPEG	JPEG
keyword	das Schlüsselwort, das reserviertes Wort
listserv	listserv
login	login Name
logon	logon
logoff	logoff

mailbox	der Briefkasten
mirror site	das Spiegel Server
modem	das Modem
Net	Net
netiquette	die Netikette, die Netiquette
newsgroup	die Gruppe
online	online
password	das Passwort
path	der Pfad
postmaster	der Postmaster
protocol	das Protokoll
real-time communication	die Echtzeit-Kommunikation
search engine	Search-Engine
search tool	die Suchhilfe
server	der Server
shell access	der Zugriff auf die Schell
snail mail	die Schneckenpost
subject directory	das Begriffs-Verzeichnis
surf	surfen (v)
synchronous communication	die synchrone Verbindung, die synchrone Kommunikation
TCP/IP	TCP/IP
telnet	das Telnet
text index	Index
thread	Thread
URL	URL
Usenet	Usenet
username	die Benutzername
Veronica	Veronica
virtual	virtuell
WAIS	WAIS
Web, WWW	das Web, das World Wide Web, das weltweite Netz, W3
Web browser	der Web-Browser
Web site	die Web-Seite
wired	vernetzt

Spanish

ENGLISH	SPANISH
@	la arroba
. (dot)	el punto
/ (forward slash)	la raya
alias	alias
anonymous FTP	el FTP anónimo
Archie	Archie
archive	el archivo
article	el artículo
ASCII	ASCII
bandwidth	el ancho de banda
BBS	el tablón de anuncios electrónicos
bookmark	el marcalibros
bookmark list	la lista de marcalibros
browser	el navegador, el browser; hojear, browsear, curiosear (v)
bug	el fallo, el bicho, el gazapo, el error
click	hacer clic, cliquear (v)
client	el cliente
command	la orden, el mandato, el comando
cyberspace	el ciberespacio
dialog box	la ventana de diálogo, cuadro de diálogo
digital	digital
direct access	el acceso directo
directory	el directorio
domain name	el nombre de dominio
download	bajar, descargar, hacer un download (v)
electronic mail	el correo electrónico
email	el email, el imail
email address	la dirección de correo electrónico
embedded hyperlink	el enlace intercalado, enlace (conexión) empotrado
emoticon	el emoticon
FAQ	FAQ (preguntas más frecuentes)
file	el archivo (de datos)

flame	el desahogo
freeware	el freeware, los programas de dominio público
FTP	FTP (Protocolo de Transferencia de Ficheros)
GIF	GIF (formato gráfico)
Gopher	el Gopher
hacker	el pirata
hardware	el hardware
hit	el impacto
homepage	la página de bienvenida, la pág. de entrada, la pág. de presentación, la pág. principal, la pág. inicial, el homepage
host	el sistema central
HTML	HTML
HTTP	el protocolo HTTP
hyperlink	el ultraenlace, el hiperenlace
hypermedia	la hipermedia
hypertext	el hipertexto
indirect access	el acceso indirecto
Internet	el (la) Internet
IRC	el IRC (charla interactiva internet)
ISP	el Proveedor de Servicios Internet
keyword	la palabra clave
listserv	el servidor de listas, la lista de correos, las listas de distribución
login	el login, hacer el login (v)
mailbox	la casilla electrónica, el casillero electrónico
modem	el módem
Net	la Red
netiquette	la etiqueta de la Red
netizen	el/la ciuredano/a
newsgroup	grupo informativo
online	en línea
password	el password, la contraseña, el código secreto
protocol	el protocolo

real-time communication	la comunicación en tiempo real
remote login	la conexión remota
search engine	el buscador, motor de búsqueda
search tool	la herramienta de búsqueda
server	el servidor
shareware	la programática compartida, el shareware
shell	el intérprete de comandos
snail mail	el correo de caracol
software	el software
surf	surfear (v)
TCP/IP	TCP/IP
telnet	el telnet, telnetear (v)
thread	el hilo
under construction	en construcción, en desarrollo
URL	el Localizador Uniforme de Recursos
Usenet	Usenet
username	el nombre de usuario
Veronica	Veronica
virtual	virtual
WAIS	WAIS
Web, WWW	el Web, la telaraña, la malla mundial
Web page maker	el tejedor de Web
Webpage	la página Web

Annotated Bibliography

INTERNET GUIDEBOOKS

There are already hundreds of Internet guides in the stores and many more on the way. As always, you will need to do a little comparison shopping before you find a guide that suits your knowledge and skill level. If you are relatively new to the Internet, it is probably best to choose a guide that explains computer concepts in nontechnical language and gives plenty of concrete examples. You will need to assess your level of interest as well. Do you want to develop your own Web site, or are you primarily interested in visiting sites? In general, newcomers to the Web should become familiar with the Web—its aesthetic, social, and technical conventions—before aspiring to produce their own Web pages. When choosing a guidebook, be sure to skim the preface and the table of contents for a better picture of the book's intended audience. Here are a few particularly useful guides for the computer novice.

The New Internet Navigator by Paul Gilster. 1997. New York: John Wiley & Sons.

The Web Navigator by Paul Gilster. 1997. New York: John Wiley & Sons.

> These best-selling guides are both extremely readable and complete. They provide an excellent introduction to the world of cyberspace.

The Internet for Dummies (4th edition) by John Levine, Carl Baroudi, and Margaret Levine Young. 1997. Foster City, CA: IDG Books Worldwide.

> Part of the popular how-to series "for dummies" written in a breezy, humorous style, this guide is chock-full of tips and warnings.

Internet and World Wide Web Simplified by Paul Whitehead and Ruth Maran. 1997. Foster City, CA: IDG Books Worldwide.

> One of the real benefits of this book is that it shows you the basics of the Internet with copious photos and drawings. If you're a visual learner, this is the book for you.

How to Use the World Wide Web (2nd edition) by Wayne Ause, Scott Arpajian, and Kathy Ivers. 1997. Emeryville, CA: Ziff-Davis Press, Inc.

> The authors of this guide compare various browsers and show you where and how to find the Web's most exciting sites.

The Internet for Busy People (2nd edition) by Christian Crumlish. 1997. Berkeley, CA: McGraw-Hill.

> Another best-selling guide—it is written for novices who want to learn how to use the Internet ASAP.

Teach Yourself the Internet in 24 Hours by Noel Estabrook. 1997. Indianapolis: Samsnet.

> This is a guide that will get you connected in record time. It contains clear exposition and good graphics.

SELECTED FOREIGN LANGUAGE RESOURCES

Arabic

Abed's Home Page—includes information about Islam and Arabic as well as links to many other Arabic language Web sites
<http://darkwing.uoregon.edu/~alquds/>

Welcome to Palestine—excellent site for cultural and linguistic information about the region
<http://www.palestine-net.com/>

University of Pennsylvania's Arabic Lessons—Arabic language course with downloadable sound files, QuickTime movie clips, and various images of the Arabic-speaking world
<http://philae.sas.upenn.edu/Arabic/arabic.html>

Arabic Mailing Lists—University of Oregon's Yamada Language Guides' Arabic mailing lists
<http://babel.uoregon.edu/yamada/lists/arabic.html>

Arabic Usenet Newsgroups—University of Oregon's Yamada Language Guides' list of Arabic newsgroups
<http://babel.uoregon.edu/yamada/news/arabic.html>

Chinese

Learn Chinese—Audio tutorial of survival Chinese with excellent audio files of words and expressions. Sound files can be played using Sound Machine for Macintosh and GoldWave for Windows.
<http://www.indiana.edu/~chasso/auchinese.html>

China News Digest—News of China from several different sources in both English and Chinese including Hua Xia Wen Zhai, the world's first comprehensive Chinese language online magazine. Regular issues are published every Friday. Includes searchable archives for both articles and photos.
<http://www.cnd.org:8023/>

Voice of America Intermediate Chinese Lessons—Voice of America (VOA) is a federally funded program of the U.S. government whose goals are to broadcast international news in many different languages. Each week, VOA adapts a news-report broadcast in Chinese for pedagogical purposes. The broadcast is presented in a series of individual sound clips with corresponding transcript material, pinyin transliteration, an English-language synopsis, and vocabulary lists with word definitions. The creators of this site warn potential users that "no grammatical tips or tutorials are provided, so this site is best used as supplementary resource material for a regular language course or self-study program."
<http://www.webcom.com/ocrat/voa/>

Chinese Mailing Lists—Yamada Language Guides' list of Chinese mailing lists

    <http://babel.uoregon.edu/yamada/lists/chinese.html>

Chinese Usenet Newsgroups—Yamada Language Guides' list of Chinese newsgroups

    <http://babel.uoregon.edu/yamada/news/chinese.html>

French

Yahoo! France—the French version of the most famous Web directory; the place to start your tour of the French Web

    <http://www.yahoo.fr/>

Lokace—the premier search engine of the Francophone Web

    <http://lokace.iplus.fr/>

Page de l'Hexagone—a master list of French links from Cornell University's Department of Modern Languages

    <http://instruct1.cit.cornell.edu/~agl1/Hexagone.html>

TennesseeBob's Famous French Links—famous among French-language teachers worldwide as one of the biggest and best directories for French links, including a superior list of online French-language resources

    <http://www.utm.edu/departments/french/french.html>

The French Studies Web—according to its creators at New York University, this site has been designed "to provide access to scholarly resources in French Studies." Coverage includes France, and the Francophone regions in Belgium, Canada, and Switzerland. The carefully selected resources are thematically grouped and liberally annotated.

    <http://www.nyu.edu/pages/wessfrench/index.html>

Canadiana—the place to go for the latest information and statistics about French-speaking Canada

    <http://www.cs.cmu.edu/Unofficial/Canadiana/LISEZ.html>

Le Web en France—a guide to Web servers in France maintained by the Centre National de Recherche Scientifique

    <http://www.urec.cnrs.fr/France/web.html>

WebMuseum, Paris—a virtual Louvre showcasing the most famous French works of art from the Middle Ages to the present. Includes special exhibits such as a recent homage to the work of Paul Cézanne

    <http://sunsite.unc.edu/louvre/>

MétéoFrance—up-to-the-minute weather reports of France and the world, including satellite images, streamed video, and, of course, forecasts

    <http://www.meteo.fr/>

French Mailing Lists—Yamada Language Guides' list of French mailing lists

    <http://babel.uoregon.edu/yamada/lists/french.html>

French Usenet Newsgroups—Yamada Language Guides' list of French newsgroups
    <http://babel.uoregon.edu/yamada/news/french.html>

German

Yahoo! Deutschland—the German version of the famous Web directory
    <http://www.yahoo.de/>

Deutschland Nachrichten—a daily German news service maintained by Yahoo! Deutschland
    <http://www.yahoo.de/schlagzeilen/>

Deutsche Welle Online—links to German newspapers, television, and radio
    <http://www.dwelle.de/>

German Studies Trails—a series of German language and culture courses (language and civilization, science and technology, arts and humanities) from the University of North Carolina—Greensboro
    <http://www.uncg.edu:80/~lixlpurc/german.html>

Germanic Languages—University of Wisconsin—Madison site with Dutch and German resources
    <http://polyglot.lss.wisc.edu/lss/lang/germanic.html#German>

German City Guide—City.Net's amazing guide to the major cities of Germany; includes up-to-date travel and entertainment information as well as maps and weather reports
    <http://www.city.net/countries/germany/>

Netzspiegel—provides students and teachers of German with "focused Internet exercises that amplify textbooks and grammar companions for basic German courses"
    <http://www.uncg.edu/~lixlpurc/NetzSpiegel/Netzspiegel.html>

German Mailing Lists—Yamada Language Guides' list of German mailing lists
    <http://babel.uoregon.edu/yamada/lists/german.html>

German Usenet Newsgroups—Yamada Language Guides' list of German newsgroups
    <http://babel.uoregon.edu/yamada/news/german.html>

Italian

Italian Home Page—excellent guide to Italian online resources from the University of Chicago's Romance Languages Resource Page
    <http://humanities.uchicago.edu/romance/italian/>

Italian Resources—Southern Methodist University's impressive list of Italian Web sites
    <http://fllc.smu.edu/languages/Italian.html>

Italian Online Newspapers—a complete list of Italian newspapers currently available on the Internet with a searchable index
<http://www.mediainfo.com/ephome/npaper/nphtm/e-papers/e-papers.italy.html>

Italian Literature Links—Infoseek's directory of Italian literature on the Web
<http://www.infoseek.com/Italian_literature?lk=noframes&svx=related>

CyberItalian—the Italian language learning site complete with grammar lessons, chat rooms, and art galleries
<http://cyberitalian.com/>

Italiano per chi viaggia—Travlang's Italian for Travelers site. Includes high quality audio files of survival Italian
<http://www.travlang.com/languages/cgi-bin/langchoice.cgi?page=main&lang1=english&lang2=italian>

Italian Mailing Lists—Yamada Language Guides' list of Italian mailing lists
<http://babel.uoregon.edu/yamada/lists/italian.html>

Italian Usenet Newsgroups—Yamada Language Guides' list of Italian newsgroups
<http://babel.uoregon.edu/yamada/news/italian.html>

Japanese

Japanese Information—this appropriately named site has information about all aspects of modern Japan
<http://www.ntt.co.jp/japan/>

The Japanese Language Research Center—contains an impressive bibliography of articles about the Japanese language written in Japanese, Japanese language attitudes studies, and links to corpora of spoken Japanese
<http://www.age.or.jp/x/oswcjlrc/index-e.htm>

Traveler's Japanese With Voice—a Japanese pronunciation guide with sound files of useful expressions
<http://www.ntt.co.jp/japan/japanese/>

WWW Servers in Japan—an annotated list of Japanese servers
<http://www.ntt.co.jp/SQUARE/www-in-JP.html>

Japanese Mailing Lists—Yamada Language Guides' list of Japanese mailing lists
<http://babel.uoregon.edu/yamada/lists/japanese.html>

Japanese Usenet Newsgroups—Yamada Language Guides' list of Japanese newsgroups
<http://babel.uoregon.edu/yamada/news/japanese.html>

Portuguese

Cadê—a Brazilian Web directory and search engine to help you untangle the Lusophone Web, similar to Yahoo!
  <http://cade.com.br/>

De Tudo Um Pouco—Glasgow University's Portuguese Link Page and language course for beginners
  <http://www.arts.gla.ac.uk:80/PortLang/>

Literatura Portuguesa—beautiful site devoted to the study of Portuguese literature with large database of texts online
  <http://www.ipn.pt/opsis/litera/>

The Portuguese Language—an overview of the language's history and dialects, including sound files and bibliography
  <http://www.leca.ufrn.br/~adelardo/portuguese/>

Portuguese Mailing Lists—Yamada Language Guides' list of Portuguese mailing lists
  <http://babel.uoregon.edu/yamada/lists/portuguese.html>

Portuguese Usenet Newsgroups—Yamada Language Guides' list of Portuguese newsgroups
  <http://babel.uoregon.edu/yamada/news/portuguese.html>

Russian

Friends and Partners—"a community of people all over the world who provide information and communications services to promote better understanding, friendship and partnership between individuals and organizations of the United States (and, more broadly, 'the west') and countries of the former Soviet Union"
  <http://www.friends-partners.org/friends/home.htmlopt-tables -mac-english->

Dazhdbog's Grandchildren—an eclectic assortment of multimedia resources about Russian history, culture, and literature
  <http://sunsite.oit.unc.edu/sergei/Grandsons.html>

SovInformBureau—the creator of this site claims that it is the "ultimate source of information on things Cyrillic, Russian, and Soviet." Well-designed links and expert advice and tools to Russify your computer.
  <http://www.siber.com/sib/>

Russian links page—a useful list of links from the MIT Russian club
  <http://anxiety-closet.mit.edu:8001/activities/russian-club /links.html>

Russian Mailing Lists—Yamada Language Guides' list of Russian mailing lists
  <http://babel.uoregon.edu/yamada/lists/russian.html>

Russian Usenet Newsgroups—Yamada Language Guides' list of Russian newsgroups

<http://babel.uoregon.edu/yamada/news/russian.html>

Spanish

Olé—the Web's premier Spanish guide and search engine

<http://www.ole.es/>

Mexsearch—a guide to Mexican Web sites

<http://www.acir.com.mx/>

Spanish Page—University of Chicago's excellent list of Spanish language links; news, literature, language courses, sports, entertainment, tourism—they're all here

<http://humanities.uchicago.edu/romance/spanish/>

Spanish Internet Resources—a large directory of Spanish links maintained by the Language Resource Center at the University of Tennessee. All links are well annotated and organized by categories: teaching tools, guides and directories, reference works, grammar and vocabulary lessons, reading, multimedia, newspapers, history, art, music, culture, cinema, food and recipes, transportation, maps and weather, and government.

<http://funnelweb.utcc.utk.edu/~doral/spanish/spanish3.htm>

Tecla—a magazine written for learners and teachers of Spanish, produced by the Spanish Department at Birkbeck College (University of London) and the Consejería de Educación, Embajada de España en Londres

<http://www.brookes.ac.uk/sol/home/resource/sp/snet.html>

Museo Picasso Virtual—a digital archive of scanned images of Picasso's art as well as a thorough bibliography containing references about the artist's life and work

<http://www.tamu.edu/mocl/picasso/>

Sí, España—an information service of the Spanish government's Dirección General de Relaciones Culturales del Ministerio Español de Asuntos Exteriores with versions in English, German, and French

<http://www.DocuWeb.ca/SiSpain/spanish/index.html>

Spanish Mailing Lists—Yamada Language Guides' list of Spanish mailing lists

<http://babel.uoregon.edu/yamada/lists/spanish.html>

Spanish Usenet Newsgroups—Yamada Language Guides' list of Spanish newsgroups

<http://babel.uoregon.edu/yamada/news/spanish.html>

Acknowledgments

Excite, WebCrawler, and the WebCrawler Logo are trademarks of Excite, Inc. and may be registered in various jurisdictions. Excite screen display copyright © 1995–1997 by Excite, Inc. (pages 46, 47, 53, 54, 94, 110)

Reprinted with full permission of The Web of Culture. Copyright 1997. All rights reserved. For more information, contact The Web of Culture at webmaven @worldculture.com, or visit our website at: www.worldculture.com. (page 81)

LANIC homepage reproduced with the permission of the Institute of Latin American Studies, University of Texas at Austin. Copyright University of Texas at Austin. All rights reserved. (pages 29, 30, 32–35)

On-line Grammars and an Index of On-Line Dictionaries reproduced with the permission of R. Beard and Bucknell University. (pages 23, 26, 27, 28)

Index